SPIRITUAL GEMS
FROM ABOVE

Spiritual GEMS from Above

Insights into Inner Peace and Joy

NEMSY GUBATAN

XULON PRESS

Xulon Press
2301 Lucien Way #415
Maitland, FL 32751
407.339.4217
www.xulonpress.com

Printed in the United States of America.

ISBN-13: 978-1-54564-904-6

Acknowledgments

$\mathcal{W}$riting this book was a challenge. There was a point when I almost gave up. But I realized that "love unlocks doors that were not even there before." It was a matter of love, I surmised—love for the Master, the good Lord—that would propel me to finish this manuscript. Therefore, with open and grateful heart, I acknowledge the hand of God in this project.

To my humble, intuitive pillar of encouragement, my wife, Perla: I relish her admonition that love is not love if it is not extravagant or heroic. She made me feel like a champion as I wrote this book.

To my wonderful and supportive children, Portia, Noel, and Neme, who espoused and lived the maxim: Life has no meaning without a strong family relationship—they were a spiritual compass pointing to what the good Lord intended for me and his people. This concept helped me include the idea in this book as it relates to our relationship with the Father.

To my Novena, Adoration and Padre Pio prayer group at church, who keyed on the principle taught by Maximillian Kolbe: All progress is spiritual or else it is not progress. Their faithfulness and support helped me to be bold and consistent in my spiritual outreach in this manuscript.

Finally, to my Filipino Christian brothers and sisters in Orlando and in the San Francisco Bay Area, who witnessed to the truth: When you are in love with the Lord, it is easy to do good and be good. Their unselfish prayers and goodwill has kept me unbridled by fear and doubt, thus inspiring me to move forward.

Introduction

*G*rowing in spirituality can be an enigma. There are so many religious paths and guru's out there proposing attractive concepts and approaches. But when I settled on Jesus, the Son of God, as the Master of my soul and my Rabbi/teacher, choosing spiritual gems in the Christian treasure chest became delightful.

The most intriguing spiritual gem is the concept of mystical union. This means the transcendence of God's love in a person's life. This means a kind of spiritual indwelling of the Divine in the human heart. This also means the inseparability of two loving hearts who are joined by the Spirit. However, without a personal encounter with the transcendent God, this spiritual union can never be achieved.

Paul, the apostle to the gentiles, had this encounter with the transcendent Jesus of Nazareth on his way to Damascus. The encounter has changed his life forever. He became more insightful and willing to share the truths about God. Similarly, my encounter with the Nazorean after my deportation trial in San Francisco, has also changed my life forever. This encounter, I have tried to sketch in this manuscript. It made me come to realize that in God's world, in God's time and space, there is never a moment when he is not in control. Since then, I became conscious of the reality that Divine Providence or God's mighty pen, is writing the story of my life. The Lord knows when to put a coma, an exclamation point, or a period in the story of my life; all I need to do is to surrender to his authorship.

Another spiritual gem is the concept of inseparability with the One we love, the Nazorean. This concept becomes clear in the words of Jesus who said, "I shall be with you always, even unto the end of the world." This was his last promise and teaching before he ascended to heaven.

Now even in the days of King David, the author of Psalm 139, has already placed a stake on this concept of inseparability. He wrote, and I selectively paraphrase, "Lord, you search me and you know me. You know my resting and my rising. It was you who created me into being. It was you who knit me together in my mother's womb. Where can I go from your Spirit? Where can I flee from your face? If I climb the heavens you are there, if I lie in my grave you are there. If I take the wings of the dawn, if I dwell at sea's farthest end, even there your hand would lead me, even there your right hand would hold me."

Eventually, the apostle Paul, caught up with this concept of inseparability with the Son of God. In Romans 8, he declared, and I selectively paraphrase, "Nothing can separate us from the love of God. Neither death nor life, neither angels or heavenly powers, neither the present or the future, neither the world above or the world below, nothing in all creation, can separate us from the love of God, which is ours through Christ our Lord." I have no doubt that this single truth, this spiritual gem, has propelled Paul to face death with utter peace and equanimity in the hands of his executioner.

There are many more spiritual gems in this humble manuscript. What's amazing is that each Christian believer would have discovered their own spiritual treasure as they ponder this book. Sharing these gems with others can help us grow in the love and service of Christ Jesus our Lord.

Nemsy Gubatan
Permanent Deacon

Table of Contents

Table of Contents

Abba

One time, I was in the mood for solitude and reflection. I decided to simply spend some time in the quiet of the early morning dawn alone in my room. First thing I did was to invoke the presence of God and simply speak to him. Of course, this was not unusual. I have done this before. Getting to know God and to converse with him would always fill me with joy and inner peace. However, this morning, I was a little bit more daring in my conversation. I asked the good Lord in a childlike way for a personal favor and inquired about his very nature and character.

The exchange was in the medium of mental prayer, reflection, and some intermittent vocal utterances on my part. There were no audible responses from God. It was all in the realm of a loving heart-to-heart exchange. In this mode, there was a sense of trust, transparency, and total acceptance of one another. When God spoke, it was simply a flash of deep insight spoken in my heart. Without trying to be precise, but simply capturing the essence of the conversation that day, this is what came up in my conversation with Abba, God the Father.

Nemsy, "Abba—Jesus, your only Son, told me to call you Abba, or Dad. I love it. And Jesus told me to get to know you better in a personal way to deepen my spirituality. So here I am, hoping to get to know you more."

Abba: Silence.

Nemsy, "You know that my earthly father died many years ago, so I would appreciate it if you can fill in his place. I never really felt the love of my earthly father, although I have longed for it so much. When Jesus told me that I can come to you as my father, I got excited. Here I am, Dad, asking you to be my father. Will you be my father?"

Abba, "Yes. I would delight in it."

Nemsy, "Wow! Thank you, Dad. I am so happy. I am happy that you sent your only Son to redeem me and then to point to you as my Father. No wonder he taught us the "Our Father" to introduce you to us as our Abba or Dad. Jesus also told us that you, Father, and Jesus are one, and that if I loved your only begotten Son, it would please you. Also, that if I loved Jesus, you would love me even more. Wow! I am surrounded by love. I am so happy."

Abba, Silence

Nemsy, "I know, Dad, that you are love, and that you have no beginning and no end. Therefore, love has no beginning and no end. But the concept of "no beginning and no end" is hard for me to understand. Can you help me?"

Abba, "You will not understand it because you are finite. When you pass from this world to the next, then you will understand. But love is infinite. Therefore, focus on love, and you will understand the answer to your question better. Love will also reveal the very nature and character of the Godhead."

Nemsy, "Thank you, Dad. I will try to focus on love."

Abba, "Yes. Focus on love, and you will be happy. Keep in mind that I made you for myself. I made you for divine intimacy, and I made you for the Kingdom."

At this point in my solitude and reflection, I began to reminisce about my earlier encounter with love. I recall that when I was a child, the first encounter I had with love was with my mother. Even for just a moment, I could not bear to be away from her loving arms. I was so possessive of my mother's love, but then I realized that I had two sisters, so I had to share my mother's love with them.

In high school, I had the usual experience of "puppy love." It was somewhat superficial, but it was an innocent love. It passed away like the fragrance of a rose. Later, after graduating from college, I began looking for my true love: someone I could call my spouse. When a good friend of mine found his true love, I was jealous. He was bragging about how it changed his life. My friend was full of life, vigor, and anticipation. When we were together, all he talked about was how happy he was because he was in love.

This manuscript is dedicated to the pursuit of practical and transforming spirituality to find inner peace and happiness. Let's call these tenets spiritual gems, or jewels. This book consists of a series of essays and anecdotes based on my personal experience and reflection on love and Divine Providence that can lead to transformation and inner peace. It uncovers my discoveries about Jesus and God the Father. In the beginning, it will reflect the truth that we all need a Savior, but we also need a Father. Why? Because we need to experience the love of Abba, our Dad, which is inborn and hardwired in us; we need to realize that everything is cradled in the arms of the Father. In fact, the reality is that, to be made whole, we need to experience the love of the most Holy Trinity: Father, Son, and Holy Spirit.

In this manuscript, you will find my encounter with the "Chaperon," or my future partner in life, and a winding and challenging love story that finally concludes in marriage. The essays related to this personal experience are coded as "Chaperon." Likewise, intertwined in this narrative is my personal encounter with the invisible and loving God who changed my life forever.

Abba's Delight

$\mathcal{S}$ome theologians believe that the New Testament verse John 3:16 is the center of the scriptures. It talks about the love and generosity of God the Father. "Yes, God so loved the world that he gave his only Son, that whoever believes in him may not perish but may have eternal life." Here, the Father lovingly gives his only Son to the world for its redemption. Subsequently, the Son sacrifices his own life to accomplish this purpose. The generous love of the Father and the Son made it possible for us to inherit the Kingdom of God, or heaven.

In my life, it was Jesus' love that I first encountered. This was manifest through my conversion experience in San Francisco. It was the result of a powerful divine intervention when the good Lord saved me and "the chaperon" from being deported back to the Philippines. I have never seen a more powerful intervention by Jesus.

As I have previously narrated, the Lord Jesus hinted that it was now time for me to know the Father, Abba, in a personal and loving way, and to call Him Abba or Dad. He reminded me that my earthly father, who had passed away many years ago, had neglected to show me a father's love and attention. Jesus was right, so it was time for me to experience the love of my heavenly Father. After all, Jesus said in Matthew 11:27, "Everything has been given to me by my Father. No one knows the Son but the Father; and no one knows the Father but the Son; and anyone whom the Son wishes to reveal."

At the time, I was convinced that Jesus wanted to reveal the Father to me in a personal way. I opened my heart and savored the words of Jesus in John 16:27; "The Father already loves you, because you have loved me, and have believed that I come from God." For me, this was indeed a giveaway. Why? Because I already loved the Son of God and I had a strong feeling that Abba already delights in me; all I had to do was to love him back. The image of a little boy and his loving disposition quickly comes to mind.

Little Johnnie loved his dad so much, and his dad loved him beyond his comprehension. Around 6 p.m. each day, Johnnie knew that his dad would be coming home from work. Therefore, as early as 5 p.m., he would play and hang around the living room, so he would be the first one to greet his dad. Then at 6 p.m., when the door opens, little Johnnie runs as fast as he could to his father, screaming, "Daddy, daddy, daddy!" At that point, Johnnie would embrace his dad's legs as tight as he could, crying out, "Daddy, take me home! Take me home."

Of course, Johnnie was already home, but what was his intention?

Well, what he really wanted was for his Dad to pick him up, carry him in his strong, loving arms, and take him inside the house. Little Johnnie's desire and longing is that his Dad would pick him up. Ah, to be carried in the arms of a loving father; for Johnnie, that was heavenly. That was unspeakable joy. However, surreptitiously, his Dad also delighted in picking up little Johnnie. Why? Because it reinforced his fatherhood. He was happy to be a father, to be a loving Dad. God the Father, Abba, our Dad, delights in picking us up when we run towards Him like a little child.

St. Therese of Lisieux, the little flower, loves this image a lot; her running to Abba's arms like a little child, and being picked up by Him. During this encounter, there is perfect giving and receiving of pure love. Usually, in

8

this posture, all fear fades away. When this happens, we find inner peace and perfect joy. This Father-Child relationship brings infinite goodness and worth to a person.

Our Father Breaks His Silence (Part I)

*M*other Eugenia Ravasio (September 1907–August 1990), an Italian Mother General of the Congregation of Our Lady of the Apostles, was known as a visionary and a mystic of the Catholic Church. In her twelve years of missionary work in the remotest parts of Africa, Asia, and Europe, she was able to open over seventy centers, each with an infirmary, school, and church. It was she who discovered the first medicine for the cure of leprosy after extracting it from the seed of a tropical plant. In fact, she opened the "Leper's City" in the Ivory Coast of Africa. Today, it remains the world's leading center of its kind.

Her most important legacy is her personal account of her private encounter or apparition of God the Father to her in 1932. She shares this series of messages from God the Father in her mini book, *The Father Speaks to His*

Children. This book was approved by Cardinal Petrus Van Lierde, Vicar General for the Vatican City State, citing that the messages in the manuscript contain nothing against faith and morals. Prior to this approval, there was a rigorous ten-year examination of the messages by Bishop Alexandre Caillot of Grenoble, France. In conclusion, the Bishop wrote, "I declare that the supernatural and divine intervention seems to me the only logical and satisfactory explanation of the facts."

The revelations of God the Father to Mother Eugenia are not new to us. It is simply a transparent and deep expression of Abba's love for us and what he desires from us, his children. For me, I am so moved by the Father's genuine affection for us as his children. It seems obvious that the Father misses his children and wants us to love him in return.

For our purposes, I will simply cite what I think is compelling and meaningful in the Father's message. And since the manuscript has many parts, I will address it in a series of messages as Part I, Part II, etc. Perplexing to me, is that I cannot recall how I got hold of this mini book. I don't remember ordering it, except that it was in my mailbox.

In this manuscript, the Father expressed his deepest longings and desires from us his beloved children. Some are amplifications, while others are new and direct requests. Here are some of the Father's sublime messages:

"I am coming to banish the excessive fear that my creatures have of me, and to show them that my joy lies in being known and loved by my children. I am coming to make myself known just as I am, so that mankind's trust may increase together with their love for me, their Father. I feel the greatest happiness in being with my children and talking to them, like a father with his children."

In this monologue, the Father is dispelling the old notion of fear of God. He presents himself as someone who is so eager to encounter and dialogue with us his children. Perhaps he feels neglected. Perhaps the Father is love-sick for us. Abba continues his message:

"Is it possible that, having called me Father, and having shown you my love, you could find in me such a hard and insensitive heart? No, no, do not believe it. I am the best of Fathers. Come to me, come with confidence and love. Even if your sins were as repulsive as mud, your confidence and your love will make me forget them. You must love me and honor me, so that you will be judged with infinitely merciful love."

Here Abba is reaching out to those who are alienated by sin. He assures us that if we have confidence in, honor, and love Him, forgiveness will not be an issue. Why? Because he is the best of Fathers. At this point, our heavenly Father zeroes in on his greatest desire. We must listen carefully.

"No one has yet understood the *infinite desire* of my divine, paternal heart is *to be known, loved, and honored* by all men. I will be much grateful to you, assuring you eternal life, if you will do me the small favor of *honoring me as I requested.* The more you honor me, the more you will honor my Son. *If you come to know me, you will love me and my beloved Son more than you do now.*"

Obviously, this is the greatest desire the Father wants; that we get to know him, to love him, and to honor him. We must heed his desire. We must make every effort to make this happen. He is speaking to us in a personal way. Each of us must respond in such a way that we are doing Abba's holy will. To make things easy, he gives us a simple devotion to follow. He says:

"Call me by the name of Father, (Abba), and you will receive much favor from me. *I like you to spend your free time with me, so that you can console me and love me for half an hour each day.* In this way, you can be well disposed *to spread this devotion* which I have just revealed to you. Remember, I can see my children's needs, their toils and desires, and my greatest happiness lies in helping and guiding them."

At last, our Father, Abba, Dad, is revealing his aching heart to us. He spells out his greatest desire *to be known, loved, and honored* by us his children. To do this he wants us to at least *spend half an hour each day* conversing, praising, honoring, and loving him—sharing our innermost thoughts, concerns and dreams with him. Imagine our loving Father, waiting each day for us to draw closer to him and speak our minds, our hearts, and our souls to him. As Jesus has saved us from sin and opened the gates of heaven for us, he now points to the Father to experience the uniqueness of a Father's love. Jesus wants us not to neglect the Father, that as children of God we must honor him and love him. Obviously, we should obey Jesus and heed our Father's request. Doing this will make us whole, change our lives, and make our hearts sing.

Our Father Breaks His Silence (Part II)

$\mathcal{W}$e continue our meditation on the visitation and appearance of Abba, God Our Father, to the holy nun Mother Eugenia Ravasio.

Her superiors in the Congregation of Our Lady of the Apostles has recognized her capability of practicing virtue to a heroic degree. In addition, she was also awarded by the French government the highest national honor for social work, the "Couronne Civique" award.

In this series, we move on to meditate on the additional benevolent and affectionate words, Abba, our Father imparts to us. Yes, God our Father, the best of the best of all fathers, wants us to know him, honor him, love him and never neglect him. He wants us to be very close to him. That's why he said:

"If a mother loves the little being I gave her, I love him more than she does, because I created him. *If you love me and call me by the sweet name of Father (Abba or Dad), you will begin to live,* here and now, in the love and the trust which will make you happy in eternity and which you will sing in heaven in the company of the elect. Is this not a foretaste of the happiness of heaven, which will last forever?"

Note the power of simply calling God: Abba, Dad, Father. This is such a precious gesture of love and respect that he promises us to experience living in the now basking in his trust and affection. Wow! This makes my heart sing even louder. After all, he created us in his image and likeness. He is the infinite fullness of what is good, beautiful and true. He is a child's reference point and the apex of final maturation to adulthood. So why can we not be totally dependent on the Father and confide all our needs to him in total trust. Setting this aside for a moment, Abba reveals more of himself:

"Do not think of me as that frightening old man whom men depict in their pictures and books. *No, no, I am neither younger nor older than my Son and my Holy Spirit.* Because of this, I would like everybody, from the youngest to the oldest, to *call me by the familiar name of Father and friend. I will give you graces for the present and bless your future.* Come! I see that you greatly need a gentle and infinitely good Father."

Wow! What a tremendous revelation. Our Dad, our Abba, is never old, but rather always young. He humbly and lovingly exposes his longing and lovesickness for us his children. That's why *Jesus said* to the holy nun and mystic Mary of the Trinity, "The Father created you to give you the Son, who redeemed you to *give you to the Father,* and to the Holy Spirit who transforms your soul." This mystical display of infinite love I often refer to as the perfect circle love of the Holy Trinity. But at times I call it *the perfect circle of love of the family of God.* Why? Because we too are drawn by the Holy Trinity to be included in their mystical circle of love. This beautiful reality and image of our personal connection with God gives me indescribable joy.

Our Father Breaks His Silence (Part III)

Now we are coming to the final words of God the Father, our Abba and Dad, as related to Mother Eugenia Ravasio's mystical experience. Take these loving words of God the Father as his parting words to us. Note how eager Abba is to hear from us and to interact with us, in order to bring us hope and peace. He said:

"I want you to be witnesses of my infinite and merciful love. I want to open my heart to you . . . let this spring gush forth and make it pass through my Son's heart to reach you. My Son Jesus is in me and I am in him, *in our interchanging love which is the Holy Spirit,* who keeps us united in this bond of love to make us one. So, come to me through my Son, *and once you are close to me, confide your desires to me."*

The word witness is invoked by the Father. For me, the message is that, as we witness for Jesus we should likewise witness for the Father. We must let the world know of our loving Father in heaven. The two are inseparable, the Son and the Father. In most cases, we are first attracted to our Savior, the one who suffered and died for our redemption. Once we are bonded with Jesus, our brother, it is not surprising that Jesus would point to the Father as the head of the family of God. This is clearly manifested in Jesus teaching us the "Our Father" prayer. Obviously, to neglect the Father in our witness, is to make our witness weak. As Jesus said, "No one comes to me unless the Father draw him." In some profound and mysterious ways, God the Father is animating the perfect circle of divine love, which is the family of God, centered in the Holy Trinity.

As an incentive, the Father gives us a magnificent promise when we answer his call to propagate devotion to his Divine Fatherhood. He said:

"And to you who will work for my glory and commit yourselves to making me known, honored and loved, I give the assurance that your reward will be great, because I will count everything, even the smallest

effort you make, and I will reward you a hundredfold in eternity."

Until the Persons (of the Holy Trinity) are honored by a special devotion in the Church, there will be something lacking in this society. Now my hour has come. Come, come closer to me; you have every right to approach your Father. *Open your hearts, pray to my Son that he may help you know even better my goodness towards you.*"

Note that God the Father invites us *to pray to Jesus to help us get to know the Father better*. This reminds me of the moment, while I was in prayer, when Jesus pointed to the Father, and encouraged me to have a close and personal relationship with Abba. At first blush, I was surprised. I knew that praying to Jesus was also praying to the Father. Still, later, I realized that although *they are one, they are not one and the same*. There is a kind of unique spiritual joy and euphoria derived in our relationship with Abba. There is this natural hunger for a Father's love. That's why Abba said to Mother Eugenia, "I will lighten their burden and sweeten their hard life. *I will inebriate them with my Fatherly love,* to make them happy in time and eternity."

Hopefully, at this point we are probably motivated to share the truths, goodness, and the power of the Fatherhood of God. Nonetheless, Abba gives us a practical consideration regarding our witnessing approach. He said:

"With regards to the means of honoring me as I desire, all I ask of you is great confidence . . . trust in me as children do. *Do not think I want austerities or mortifications.* I do not want you to walk barefoot or to lay your faces in the dust, or to cover yourselves with ashes. No, No! *My dearest wish is that you behave as my children, simply trusting in me . . . and to show my sole desire; to love you and be loved in return by you. I will always show myself to be your Father, provided that you show yourself to be my children. It is through my Son and the Holy Spirit that I am coming to you, and it is in you that I seek my repose.*"

Note the sincere desire of Abba to be loved back. And we must do so, we must love the Father back. We cannot be ungrateful. And why not? Remember that the Father is a father because he has children. And we his children are indeed children, because we have a loving

Father. This is the natural order. We as God's children, were created as children so we can love back our Father. To subvert this natural order is grave error.

This ends our three-part series on the Father's lament and wishes. Hopefully we will assimilate this messages and put it into practice. In some direct way, it invites us to give some tender and loving attention to God our Father. Perhaps we have taken Abba's love and desires for granted. Perhaps we have never been aware of it. Perhaps no one has ever mentioned this divine longing of our heavenly Father for intimacy. But now we have been awakened by his openness, transparency and lovesickness. Let us be conscious in building a relationship with the Father. Let us get to know him and bond with him. Most of all let us enjoy his Fatherhood—his being our Abba, our Dad.

How I wish I had known this in my younger days. Those days when I needed most an earthly father's love. But thanks be to God, Jesus, my Lord and Savior, took upon himself to take care of my physical and emotional needs. And when the time was ripe, the Son of God pointed to Abba as my heavenly Father. What a perfect gift, now my spiritual journey will be much more pleasant and enjoyable. Suddenly, the words I hear during the liturgy, as intoned by the priest, "Through him (Jesus), and with him, and in him, *O God, almighty Father,* in the unity of the Holy Spirit, *all glory and honor is yours,* forever and ever. Amen."

Stealing the Heart of Jesus

There is an ancient legend about a Carmelite monk named Macarios who lived on top of a mountain—he was known for his wisdom and holiness. As such many people from far and near would venture to see him for advice.

One day a spiritual seeker named Albert dared to climb the mountain to see and consult with the old monk. Arriving, he greeted the old monk and said, "Master, you look pretty well settled in this peaceful place, do you still wrestle with the devil?"

The old monk smiled and replied, "Not as much anymore my son. I'm getting old and tired, and the devil is also getting tired of me—so he leaves me alone."

"Well, is it a lot easier for you now, Master?" Albert piped in.

The Master paused and said, "Not really. When I was young, I used to wrestle with the devil a lot. But now that I am older, I wrestle with God—and it is a lot, lot harder."

With a bit of excitement, Macarios exclaimed, "So you wrestle with God—and you hope to win?"

"No, I wrestle with God and hope to lose so I can be reformed and transformed by his mercy and love. In this way, he wins, and I win too," Macarios gently replied.

What an insight by the old Master: Let God win, let him have his way, and in so doing we can be magnificently changed and transformed into his image and likeness.

In our lives, it is easy to remember how we wrestled with the devil when we were young. There's the wrestling with the ego, with vanity, and with prestige. There's also wrestling with excessive pleasure, material possessions, and financial security. In the long run, we are faced with the question of who do we really trust—our judgement or God's admonitions? The simple answer is let God win. Let this be our first non-negotiable pattern—always trusting and having confidence in God. Why? Because as St. Paul said, "All things work together for good to those who love God." This means that if we love God and have confidence in him, in the end, things will work out for us—especially things that really matter.

One time, Jesus appeared to St. Gertrude of Germany and said to her, "The *firm confidence* a person has in me, believing that I truly can

26

help him at all times, *steals my heart,* and I cannot but favor such a soul because of the great pleasure I experience in seeing him so dependent upon me."

Without being too exaggerated, do you want to steal God's heart? Who wouldn't? It would be a blissful thing to happen to us. Nonetheless, as *Jesus said, all it takes is total trust and confidence in him.* This means *letting Jesus win* in every turn and aspect of our lives. With this humble approach, we can be truly elated and joyful.

Love Has No Fear

*I*n the annals of history, the heroic, the bold, and the audacious are admired more than silver or gold. It is the pinnacle of greatness and magnanimity. Perhaps little is known of the interior force and the "ferocious fire within" that propels one to greatness linked with the ultimate sacrifice.

In the movie "Of God's and Man," eight Cistercian monks living in Algeria are intimidated by a group of Islamic fundamentalist. In fact, the whole village is terrorized by the group—their goal was to take over the village. The monks are bewildered about leaving the monastery or staying to continue their ministry to the poor villagers. With intense prayer and contemplation, they decided to stay and continue to serve the poor. They have become fearless. Pure love of God became their shield.

One time one of the monks providing medical care to a family was asked by a young woman who was contemplating marriage, *"How do you know when you are in love?"* Reflecting, the monk replied, *"There is something in you that comes to life. He is the one you think most of the time."* With sparkling eyes, the woman whispered, "I think I will marry my suitor, I think of him most of the time."

Who do you think most of the time, or what do you think most of the time? Your answer will determine what consumes your life. If it is God you think most of the time because you love him, then he will come to life in you. Jesus, the Son of God will come to life in you. He becomes your new paragon. You will have a new life, and what a difference that can be. You will be empowered, and happiness will just be around the corner.

Obviously then, when love strikes, things change a lot. Fear melts away, and dread is suspended. There is new freedom and new assurance. You can be bold; you can take risks for the love of God. You can then embrace the greatest risk. As a mystic once said:

"To laugh is to risk appearing the fool.
To weep is to risk appearing sentimental.
To reach out for another is to risk involvement. But to risk must be taken,

because the greatest hazard in life is to risk nothing.

The people who risk nothing do nothing, have nothing, are nothing. They may avoid suffering and sorrow, but they cannot learn, feel, change, grow. Chained by their attitudes and complacency, they are slaves; they have forfeited their freedom. Only a person who risks is free. And *the greatest risk is to fall in love with God, for therein lies the greatest freedom and the greatest joy."*

Therefore, be happy; take the risk of giving your heart and your life to God. You will feel fulfilled and much happier.

Love is Life

*I*n the movie *The Hunger Games*, Katniss, a lovely lady, and Peeta, a resourceful young man, along with other young adults, were forced by the government to participate in the life-and-death gladiator games. The games were televised by the repressive government for the entertainment of the people.

In the fierce combat among the participants, Katniss and Peeta became allies for the sake of survival. As they both struggled to defend themselves against the other combatants, they developed a close relationship. In the end, against all odds, they both survived and won the games.

During the awards ceremony, in front of a large crowd, the Master of Ceremonies asked Katniss, "When did you know you had an attraction to Peeta?" She replied, "*It was when I realized I did not want to live my life without him.*"

Cleary that was the criteria, an attraction that resulted in the mingling of two lives, "I did not want to live my life without him." And yet this attraction and mingling of two lives was developed through companionship and facing adversity together.

The movie came in episodes, with Katniss and Peeta being separated because of the revolution wherein the people tried to oust the dictator. In the end, freedom was achieved, and the two lovers were reunited and got married.

I can see in the story that their love for each other gave them strength, courage and hope. As long as they were in love, they were unbeatable. As someone said, "Falling in love is like jumping off a tall building. Your mind tells you it is not a good idea, but your heart tells you, you can fly." And for Katniss and Peeta madly in love, they felt they could fly.

In the same way, *Jesus gives us this sense of invulnerability because of his love.* His pure love gives us wings to overcome the world. His mercy, like a strong wind, sustains our flight. Why? Because he loves us. As the Son of God, his sacrifice on the cross means so much to us. His promise to be with us even unto the end of this world is life giving. And for us who believe and love him, we know we cannot live without Him. *His love is our lives.* With this love, we are happy and secure.

The Chaperon

*L*ife is full of surprises. When we least expect it, the experience of a lifetime engulfs us and becomes a milestone in our lives. At first we think it is just a happy coincidence, but downstream we realize it is the hand of God. Let me share a personal story with you.

The phone rang and I grab it immediately. As expected, it was my good friend Rendy. He said, "Nemsy, there's a university dance this weekend, and I have arranged a blind date for you. She's rather charming and a good dancer. Let's meet at the usual place and go from there."

His invitation was rather timely and encouraging, because at the time I was keeping my eyes open for a possible partner in life. With eagerness, I told him that I was looking forward to meet this "blind date."

At the appointed time, we drove to meet my blind date at her residence. What would she look like? Then it happened, I was formally introduced to her and I noticed that she was upbeat and had a big smile in her face. Well dressed in a semi-formal gown, she greeted us politely. I smiled back and shook her hands. Then, without missing a beat, she said, "I forgot to tell you that I am taking a chaperon with me.

"Chaperon!" I silently mumbled under my breath. I saw my friend nervously glance at me. Without hesitation, my blind date continued, "Let me introduce her to you."

Momentarily, she disappeared and came back with her chaperon. As soon as I saw her, I was dazzled by her charm and beauty. Wearing a simple dress, she looked like royalty to me. Although somewhat shy and unassuming, I could not take my eyes away from her. As she was introduced to us, she simply smiled and did not say a word.

When we arrived at the "Tres Hermanas" grand ballroom, the party was already at full swing. That night I remember dancing with my blind date, but the one time I danced with the chaperon I felt the evening was enchanted and the whole world seem to have vanished into oblivion. My wish at the time was that the music would never end. To my surprise I sensed that she was also enjoying my company. We were laughing and exchanging pleasantries with great delight.

For me, the attraction was compelling, and I began to wonder if I was falling in love.

The days that followed confirmed what I feared most, I could not forget the chaperon. Our moments together that night, brief as it was, had captured my imagination. I made up my mind that I would see her again.

There is something magic about human love. In some small ways, it mirrors divine love. Yet, in the final analysis they are complimentary. Obviously, God is the greatest lover of all. But we are called to experience this overwhelming and intoxicating love in both human and divine love. Note however, that this posture can only lead to one thing, happiness and inner joy.

The Chaperon Pursued

*U*nable to shake away my attraction towards the chaperon, one day I mustered up all my bravado and decided to take a chance and visit her. It was a beautiful Saturday morning as I knocked at the door of her apartment where she stayed with her cousin, my previous blind date. Unconsciously, I was hoping that my previous blind date would not be around so I could chat with the chaperon alone. As the door opened I was met by an older woman. I politely asked for the chaperon and she smiled and ushered me into the living room. While waiting, I said to myself, "This must be my lucky day," as I was looking forward to seeing this "lady of my dreams."

The older woman returned and apologized telling me that the chaperon was not home. I inquired what time she would be coming home; but she simply smiled. I knew what she meant. Disappointed, I said goodbye and left the apartment. As I headed home I had the feeling that something was amiss. Why would the woman usher me to the living room and then tell me that the chaperon was not home?

The following week, I told myself that this "puppy love" was over. I kept telling myself that this fascination and infatuation was not meant to be, yet the more I was trying to convince myself of this, the more I was compelled to try and see her again. Like a revolving roulette, I kept asking the nagging question: why can't I forget the chaperon? This reminded me of what I once discovered to be true:

Love in the truest sense . . . is

a never-ending presence; it is

something you cannot hide.

Finally, I decided to give it another try to visit the chaperon again. It was another beautiful Saturday morning when I knocked at the apartment door, and the same older woman met me at the entrance. She knew I was looking for the chaperon, so she once again ushered me into the living room. As I waited, my mind was playing games. What if I am told that she is not home? What if my blind date showed up instead of the chaperon? What if both of them showed up? What if I was told never to come back again? Ah, the tenacity of enduring love; Robert Frost describes it this way:

> **"Love is an irresistible desire**
>
> **to be irresistibly desired."**

Suddenly, there she was, the chaperon, the lady of my dreams, more beautiful than ever. I could hardly say a word; but she broke the silence. "How are you? I heard you were here last week. There was a slight confusion, but all is fine now."

I told her that I was in the area, so I thought I'd pay her a visit. She smiled and we continued our conversation like the soft sound of running deer along a silver pond. It was at that moment that I realized that love must be experienced in its fullest sense to be understood. Yes, this was just the beginning, what would it be like in its prime? As Emme Bache once said:

"The past is behind us, but love is

always in front of us, and all around us

The Chaperon Left Behind

*H*aving made the initial visitation, the courtship began! It was the most exhilarating and enchanting experience of my life. Like two butterflies dancing in the wind, we took in life as we never did before. I began to understand that reason was secondary to the dictates of the heart. This is beautifully expressed by Blaise Pascal who said:

> "The heart has its reasons, that
> reason knows nothing about."

Another thing that attracted me to the chaperon, was her being a devout Catholic. She always carried her rosary and often invited me to go with her to church. And we did. As we visited different churches in Manila, I was impressed by her sincere devotion to the Virgin Mary. Somehow I sensed a spiritual connection between us, which convinced me that our relationship would last.

After six months of courtship and casual rendezvous, I was ready to settle down and marry the chaperon. But the harsh realities of life can thwart even the best of plans and intentions. Separation was on the horizon.

Out of the blue my parents decided to send me to San Francisco, California, to further my studies. They said that I had a distant "uncle" there who could help me with housing. Although I was hesitant and opposed the idea, my parents were adamant. They said I had no option. In the end, I complied.

My last rendezvous with the chaperon was extremely sad. As I broke the bad news to her, I could not bear to see the look in her face. It almost seemed to both of us that the world we knew was coming to an end. But we consoled each other, promising to correspond frequently and pursue our dream of being united forever. We said goodbye with the belief that each of us would be faithful regardless of what the future would bring. With heavy hearts, we parted with a tender embrace, and soon tears flowed like a river.

The Chaperon Waiting

*A*fter my last meeting with the chaperon, the next thing I knew I was flying to San Francisco, "the city by the bay." Ironically, I left my heart in Manila. I thought this kind of drama happened only in the movies, but experiencing the stark reality of it all was truly devastating. Landing at the airport, I then took a taxi to my uncle's house.

At this point in my shattered dream, spirituality suddenly became important. I began to appreciate the importance of prayer and the hope it generated. In the chaperon's letters, she informed me that she was earnestly praying for our reunion. For both of us, God became a welcomed third party. There were no cell phones at the time, and long distance was exorbitant, so we kept the letters going.

I enrolled at the University of San Francisco taking some business courses while on a student visa. As a foreign student, I was not allowed to work, but as time went by, money became an issue. Working part time was a temporary solution.

With all the demands of work and study, I found myself more dependent on God; praying and going to church became part of my schedule. Now distanced from my old buddies in Manila, I was amazed at how I became more disciplined and proficient in my day to day activities. As I sought the Lord, I was slowly being changed from within. The Divine Bridegroom was consoling my heart.

> **When you seek me with all your heart, you will find me with you, says the Lord, and I will change your lot. —Jeremiah 29:14**

A year went by so quickly, like the twilight shadows swallowed by the subtle darkness of the evening. Although the letters were coming every other week, the nagging desire to see the chaperon never left me. Then one day the thought of bringing her to San Francisco entered my mind. Was this divine intervention, I wondered? But I had no idea how to go about it. I knew that I had to save some money for her airfare and that I would have to find a place for us to stay.

After praying over this idea, the first thing I did was to approach my "uncle." Fortunately, he was a kind and reasonable man. As a former photographer and now a barber, he knew people of different trades. He also knew how to handle the "ins and outs" of bringing people from the Philippines to the United States.

At last, having made up my mind to give it a try, I went to his barber shop. There as I was having a haircut, I told him about my sad story and my plan to bring the chaperon to America. He smiled and said, "That's not easy, you are on a student visa, and she has no legal reason to come here." Fortunately, he noticed the disappointment and the sadness in my face, and after a long pause, he said; "But if God wants it to happen, it will happen. Let me think about it some more."

The Chaperon on the Wings of Prayer

After the meeting, I prayed more earnestly that the good Lord would help my "uncle" find a way to bring the chaperon to America. Like a singing sparrow, I kept chirping the same song to the Son of God. Somehow, I felt closer to Him and felt that He was listening. It was like a new day was dawning despite my Herculean demise.

As Hildegard of Bingen would say:

> "Don't let yourself forget that God's grace rewards not only those who never slips, but also those who bend and fall.

It was a beautiful Sunday morning when my "uncle" invited me to go out for breakfast with him. I had the feeling that he would tell me about his plan for the chaperon. As we enjoyed our breakfast, he asked me how much money I had saved; and I told him. Evidently, it was not enough; but he told me that he would help me out. I was speechless.

Then he continued, "I'm working on her visa. Keep praying that things will work out. If all goes well, she can be here within six months." I could hardly believe what I heard. My humble uncle suddenly now appeared to me as a giant of a man and an irreplaceable ally. I told him that I was forever indebted to him. As we finished our conversation, I was buoyed up by a deep sense of gratitude and hope. As Shakespeare would say:

> **"Hope is a lover's staff; walk hence with that, and manage it against despairing thoughts."**

Six months! For me it was like waiting for the next eclipse of the sun to happen. It was a long and tedious wait. Although the chaperon was thrilled to know about her coming over, our letters were filled with tremendous anticipation. In one of her letters she informed me that a travel agent directed by my uncle, contacted her about getting a tourist visa. Obviously, the logical starting place was the US Embassy in Manila where she would file the necessary papers and expect a personal interview.

The letters that followed informed me that her interview was short. It was because the American interviewer was given a birthday party by her friends. The party went a little longer, and as a result, the chaperon's interview was cut short. In fact, she was only asked one question, "Why are you going to San Francisco?" The chaperon answered, "Because I want to visit my aunt and uncle there."

At that point, she was simply asked to go get her immunization shots and file for her tourist visa. That was the last time the chaperon entered the US Embassy in Manila. In my mind, I was pondering the question, "Was the hand of God in this event, or was this pure coincidence?

Perhaps the words of Anicius Boethius, a Christian philosopher, can give us a deeper insight. He said:

> "God looks forth from the high watch-towers
>
> of his providence;
>
> he sees what suits each man, and
>
> applies to him that which suits him."

The months that followed seem to move ever so slow because my anticipation of the chaperon's arrival was so intense. It was like a nervous farmer waiting for rain to drench his barren land. Later, the chaperon told me that she tried to keep her departure to the US a guarded secret; only close friends and relatives knew about it.

On my part, I also tried to keep everything to myself; even my parents and siblings did not have a clue about what I was trying to engineer. However, there was a slight delay because of the "affidavit of support" papers required by the embassy. When I told my uncle about this, he said that he was aware of the situation and that he was working on it.

The Chaperon Emerges from the Ashes

*F*inally, the breakthrough came. I received the chaperon's letter telling me that she was finally ready to come over; she was now in possession of an airline ticket, a passport, and a visa. After six months of eager anticipation of her arrival, I was now finally given a flight number, a date, and a time of her arrival in San Francisco. At that point I was bursting with joy like an eagle finding a mountain peak where it could build its nest. Sensing that I was indebted not only to my uncle, but also to God, I stopped by a nearby church and spent some time with the Master.

The days that followed found me preparing for the arrival of the chaperon. I told my uncle about her arrival, but he already knew. With a sneaky smile, he told me, "This is what you have been waiting for. Go ahead and welcome her to San Francisco. I will join you later." At this point, I was inundated with peace and happiness coming from the depth of my soul. Perhaps Leon Blay can add meaning to this emotion. He said:

> **"Joy is the infallible sign**
>
> **of the presence of God."**

There I was at the airport terminal, thirty minutes early, and eagerly waiting. My mind was reeling with questions and with images of how she would look like. Did she cut her hair? Did she wear a simple dress or a fancy one? How much luggage did she bring? Did she enjoy her flight? How would I react when I see her? Who took her to the airport in Manila? What did her mother and brother say about her going to a foreign land? The questions were endless.

Then, like a lovely dream from the past, a shining star from a distant galaxy, I spotted her, looking and waiting for someone to fetch her. She was wearing a simple white hat, elegant and tasteful. Her blue dress was stylish with a dainty white collar arrayed with small polka dots. Her high heels were white, with a European flare. She wore a beautiful matching necklace which added dignity to her stature. For me, she looked more beautiful than ever.

I approached her slowly, and then at a distance she recognized me. Our eyes met, and I saw the expression of unbridled joy in her face. She walked towards me carrying a small luggage. Then like the pale moonlight hugging the ocean shores, we gently kissed and embraced. Fireworks! Unchained energy pulsated in my being. Time stood still, and the world vanished. Ah, the enchantment and invisible force of love. Perhaps the words of Teilhard de Chardin can bring some illumination.

> "Someday, after mastering the winds, the waves, the tides, and gravity, we shall harness for God the energies of love, and then, for a second time in the history of the world, man will have discovered fire."

From the airport, I took the chaperon to my aunt's house where she and my cousins graciously hosted us for dinner. It was a wonderful evening of laughter and endless questions. Everyone was so excited to meet the chaperon. My aunt told me later that a small place has been rented for us for a month until we have decided for ourselves where to stay. "How can God be so gracious?" I asked myself. Like a sudden burst of fresh air, everything seemed to fall in place with God's help. As I looked back into that signature day, I took it as a major milestone in my life. As Ruth Ann Schabacker would say:

> **"Each day comes bearing its own gifts. Untie the ribbons."**

The Chaperon Takes her Vows

*D*uring dinner, there was a slight discomfort in everyone's mind; the chaperon and I were not yet married. To calm down the anxiety, I announced to everyone that we will obtain a marriage license rather quickly and then follow it up with a formal wedding in church. As expected, everyone breathed a sigh of relief; and the merriment of the evening continued.

The days that followed were spent in getting a marriage license. Signing the papers were almost ceremonial, perhaps anticipating a more solemn exchange of vows in a wedding ceremony. With the marriage license acquired, it was now a delight for me to introduce the chaperon as my wife.

Eventually, the wedding came to fruition which happened at St. Kevin's Church. It was a simple but dignified ceremony. The chaperon wore a lovely white traditional wedding dress and a white tiara. I wore a plain black tuxedo with a bow tie. As she came down the aisle, lovely and charming as ever, she was like a dove ascending over the horizon to meet its mate. Deep emotions and feelings of fulfillment enveloped my consciousness. As we knelt at the altar in front of the presiding priest, surrounded by extended family and close friends, we heard the priest say to us:

"Nemsy and Perla, have you come here freely and without reservation to give yourselves to each other in marriage?"

"Yes, we have."

"Will you love and honor each other as man and wife for the rest of your lives?"

"Yes, we will."

"Will you accept children lovingly from God, and bring them up according to the law of Christ and his Church?"

"Yes, we accept."

Then the priest told us to join hands and to repeat the marriage vow after him, nodding at me first.

"I, Nemsy, take you Perla, to be my wife. I promise to be true to you in good times and in bad, in sickness and in health. I will love you and honor you all the days of my life."

Then, with intentionality, the priest looked at the bride and asked her to repeat the same vow. And she did, with almost a hushed tone, and with teary eyes.

I could not contain myself at that point, so did the people in attendance. The silence was deafening, while some older women were pulling out their handkerchiefs. Obviously, God touches the hearts of people who knows how to honor new covenants, new beginnings, and new dreams.

After the exchange of vows, came the exchange of rings. As I placed the ring in the bride's finger, I declared:

"Perla, take this ring as a sign of my love and fidelity. In the name of the Father, and of the Son, and of the Holy Spirit."

Now it was the bride's turn to place the ring in my finger, and she did, gracefully. More prayers followed, and then a final blessing. At the end of the ceremony came the final instruction, "You may kiss the bride."

Ah, the eternal kiss before man and God, joined by divine providence and sealed by a marriage vow. It doesn't get any better than this . . . happiness at its best captured in the human heart! As George Sand said:

"There is only one happiness in
life, to love and be loved."

Marching out of the church with my bride,
surrounded by friends and extended family, I
was beaming with unspeakable joy and elation.
The small reception that followed was at my
aunt's house where champagne and an abundance
of Filipino food were served. Pondering the
events of the day I knew that somehow the
hand of the God was orchestrating this happy
ending. Tomorrow did not even come to mind.
The euphoria of being in love, and an awareness
of the Lord's presence was sufficient for the
moment. Looking at the world with "enchanted
eyes" I felt a sense of contentment that all
is well, and all will be well. Perhaps the
words of James Peterson can express it in a
more meaningful way:

"If you are afraid for your future,
you don't have a present."

The Chaperon Settles Down

In my mind, I kept thinking that all that has happened to me and Perla was pre-ordained. Why pre-ordained? Because the probability of being married in the San Francisco while I was a student and Perla was a visitor was unlikely. The timing was also uncanny. The ideal scenario would be for both of us completing our studies, and for me to be gainfully employed as a US citizen. But this process would probably take many years. Yet through faith, fidelity, and prayer, the inconceivable happened. Why? Because as a mystic once said:

> After all love is a miracle, it is always
> willing to do the impossible.
> It can move mountains and reach for the
> stars. And with God, nothing is impossible.

The day after the wedding, the feeling of being a responsible husband crossed my mind. Fortunately, before Perla arrived, I have managed to switch my part-time employment to a full-time job; thanks to the abundance of job at the time. The daytime work and evening classes were challenging, but the power of love blessed by the sacrament of marriage were like the two wings of an angel sustaining our flight into family life. In all this, it was faith that glued everything together. As George MacDonald said:

> "This is a sane, wholesome, practical, working faith: That it is a man's business to do the will of God; second, that God himself takes on the care of that man; and third, that therefore that man ought never to be afraid of anything."

Indeed, faith and our mutual love was the glue that held our lives together. As we did in Manila, we attended Sunday mass together. In school, I was doing fine; and my job was likewise rewarding and promising. Still the nagging thought of my working full time worried me. What if the US Immigration and Naturalization Service (INS) discovered that I was working full time with only a student visa? I knew I needed a permit to work full time, but then I also knew that in most cases working full time while going to school was not allowed. After a soul-searching process, I decided to take the risk and bite the bullet. At that moment, I simply sighed and murmured, "At least Perla and I are together; whatever happens, we are together." And so, with acceptance of what lay ahead, I simply trusted in the One who knows all things. At this point, perhaps we can learn from Dwight Eisenhower's mother, who said:

"Boys, this is only a game. But it's like life, in that you will be dealt some bad hands. Take each hand, good or bad, and don't whine and complain, but play it out. If you're man enough to do that, God will help, and you will come out well."

Then came the endless summer. During the weekends, Perla and I would explore the gorgeous hills of San Francisco, the cable cars crawling up the hill, and the blue ocean waters surrounding the Bay Area. The majestic Golden Gate Bridge beckoned us to cross it and head for Sausalito and the surrounding winery. The evening brought us to dine in Chinatown, and before the day was over, head towards Fisherman's wharf where we would reminisce over our exciting adventures.

Each morning before going to work, I could hear the children playing in the school yard at the back of St. Philip's Catholic Church which was just half a block away from our apartment. Their voices would remind me that someday, Perla and I would also hear the voice of our firstborn child. Next to the church was the rectory where Fr. Thomas Reagan, the Pastor resides. I knew him by name only, since I was not active in any ministry in the church. Although his sermons were inspiring and challenging, my heart was not ready to assimilate his beautiful message. Being too focused in trying to be a responsible husband and a good student, I was at best, a pew warmer in the church.

The Chaperon is Troubled

*P*icking up the mail was a daily routine, except for one day when I noticed an officially looking envelope. It was from the US Immigration and Naturalization Service (INS). As I stared at the envelope, my heart skipped a beat, and I froze in my tracks. Troubling and fearful thoughts entered my mind. Entering the house, I sat on the couch and slowly opened the envelope. This reminds me of what Louis L'Amour said:

> "A man who says he has never been scared
> is either lying or else he's never
> been any place or done anything."

With trepidation, I slowly read the letter. It said something about deportation and about being required to leave the country within seven days. It mentioned about picking up our tickets at the TWA counter at the airport. The notice shattered my composure like a house rattled by a sudden earthquake. "Why now?" I mumbled. "With everything going so well, with having successfully brought Perla to America, why this deportation notice?" My mind was racing like a frightened kangaroo. Then I thought, "What about my studies, my promising job, my gentle and generous uncle who worked hard to bring Perla to America?"

Feeling helpless I simply closed my eyes and sighed, "Who can deliver me?" Like the Psalmist, I was unconsciously pleading to a higher power.

> "In you, O Lord, I take refuge; let me never be put to shame. In your justice rescue me, incline your ear to me; make haste to deliver me!" —Psalm 31:2

Hardly believing that I was now holding in my hands the letter I dreaded the most, I sat on the living room sofa calming myself down.

Taking a deep breath, I stood up, and went to see Perla who was working in the kitchen.

> **"We fear things in proportion to our ignorance of them." —Livy**

Pretending to be calm, I told her about the deportation letter. She looked at me with disbelief; she was not expecting the notice so soon. Gingerly and lovingly, she sat next to me. We held hands in silence. After some time, she looked at me and started the conversation.

"Shall I start packing our clothes? What about the furniture?"

"I don't know. Let me figure things out."

"Shall I tell anyone about this?"

"Not yet. Let me go to church right now; I feel that I need to pray."

> **"A man without prayer is like a tree without roots." —Pope Pius XII**

While walking to St. Philip's church which was only half a block away, I was scrambling for words to say to the good Lord. I knew deep in my heart that reaching out to a higher power was my only hope.

As I entered the church, I noticed that the altar was dimly lit. The whole church was partly illuminated by the sunlight streaming through the stained-glass windows. To my surprise, no one else was inside the church! It was quiet. "Ah, the children are in school, and the morning mass is over," I mumbled to myself. "What an opportune time, I am alone," I sighed with relief.

Obviously, my heart was heavy at the time, and I had so much to talk to God about. Drawn by the huge life-size crucifix above the altar, I gingerly walked towards it, and knelt. Facing the huge cross, I gazed at the image of the crucified Christ and noticed his bloodstained face. The big gaping wound on his side caught my attention . . . so did the big nails piercing his hands and feet. Realizing that no one was around, I decided to unload all my problems and anxieties before the sorrowful Redeemer. Gently, sincerely, and with reverence, I began to pray straight from the heart in my native language, Tagalog. I said something like this:

"Lord, why did this happen to me? Why now? Couldn't you have given me a little more time to prepare? I know that I have not been an ideal Christian, but perhaps I can do better in the future. I do not know how to handle this problem, it is too big for me, too complicated, and too sudden. You know my resources are limited; I do not know any big shot who can help me. How about Perla and our dreams to start a new life here? Is it about to be shattered? We were hoping to raise a family and perhaps finish my studies here. But now, what is going to happen to us? Where did I do wrong?"

As sometimes happen, when prayer becomes intense, the dialogue occurs without even being conscious of the process. As such, the Lord's answer comes like a "brain wave data transfer" or sometimes called "inner locution." The subconscious mind receives the answer and the intellect does not doubt where it is coming from, as such, the response is clear but not audible. This mode of prayer happens when our eyes are closed and the physical senses are barely operative.

A few moments later, in the deep silence of my heart I sensed the merciful Savior gently responding:

"Nemsy, you have not been serious about our relationship and about my sacrifice on the cross. You are too busy with so many things. You gaze at my crucified image, but you do not *really appreciate* what I have done for you. *Do you understand what my dying on the cross really mean?*"

I was puzzled by the question. Of course, I knew that he died on the cross for my sins and the sins of the world. But then why did he say that I did not appreciate what he has done for me. "Did I in any way take him for granted, or considered his help and support as insignificant?" I pondered this questions in my heart. I was silent. I was not prepared to respond.

As I knelt in stillness, my whole life story paraded itself before me. Like watching a movie of myself. I saw those careless and callous moments in my college days. Those carefree fraternity social gatherings. I grimaced as I watched them. Sadness gripped my heart. But then there were also those few animated, and joyful moments when I felt the invisible hand of God guiding me. What was obvious however, was my preoccupation with myself. I was always first, and the Lord was either second of third in line. It was clear, I took Him for granted, and I did not appreciate all He has done for me, even on the cross. *I did not fully understand the depth of his sacrifice.*

As I continued my self-examination, I realized that I thought of God mostly when I needed something, or when I attended Sunday mass. I felt shallow, vacillating, and ashamed. Then like a bolt of lightning, my heart was struck with sorrow and deep repentance. I began to weep.

> "True repentance has a double aspect.
> It looks upon things past with
> weeping eye, and upon the future with
> a watchful eye." —Robert Smith

Under the shadow of the cross I knelt for some time. Swept by remorse and contrition, I became fully aware of my sins and shortcomings. I was aware of my mediocre love. Then gently I uttered the following words:

"Lord, it was my fault. I have been too self-absorbed. I have offended you . . . so sorry. I deserve to be chastised and vanquished; but I continue to cling to you and depend on your mercy. Like the prodigal son, Lord Jesus, I return to you asking for mercy and forgiveness. Please, give me a second chance. Please give me a second chance."

> **"Forgiveness is the final form of love." —Reinhold Niebuhr**

After the prayer and a moment of silence, a deep, soothing peace came over me. I felt that my confession was heard. Even without a response from the Master, I sensed his merciful glance. I felt free from the ugly past. I was moved to tears.

> **"Forgiveness is the most tender part of love." —John Sheffield**

In the silence of the moment, the sweet familiar inner voice of the Master echoed in my heart:

"My child, I have heard your prayers, there is nothing more you need to worry about. I will help you and take care of the problem. Go in peace."

Hearing this, my elation was indescribable. I believed every word he said. I was about to shout, but I knew I was inside the church. A surge of energy came upon me as though meeting someone really special who has handed me a gift. I spent more time praying in front of the crucifix—prayers of gratitude, appreciation and veneration. Clear as a bell, I understood this moment as the dawning of a new day for me. "Free at last, free at last," I mumbled to myself.

"God has two dwellings, one in heaven, and the other in a thankful heart." —Anonymous

---

The Chaperon in Deportation

I walked back to our apartment. There I noticed Perla preparing to pack her clothes. I hugged her and told her that everything would be alright. She looked perplexed, so we sat down and talked.

"What happened?" she exclaimed.

"I went to talk to Jesus. I told him everything."

"So?"

"We had a long conversation. He gave me a second chance. He said not to worry because he would take care of our problem."

"Really? Did he really say that?"

"Not audibly. You know . . . you just know it in your heart."

"So what do you plan to do?"

"Well, first of all, you don't have to pack any of your clothes. We will simply wait in hope, for God's plan to unfold."

> "If it were not for hope, the heart
> would break." —Thomas Fuller

The next morning, I woke up early and said my prayers. This time it had a special ring to it. I recalled the previous day's marvelous spiritual peak experience, and the encouraging message the good Lord imparted to me. But how would he take care of my deportation problem? Can my "uncle" help me? Can the pastor of St. Philip's help me? He doesn't even know me! How about my employer, can he help me? As I pondered all these questions, I kept my hopes high. I was positive that a solution would arise, I was placing my bet on the Lord.

> "The only way to make rapid progress
> along the path of divine love is to
> remain very little and to put all our
> trust in Almighty God. That is what I
> have done." —St. Therese of Lisieu

The following morning, there was a knock on the door. "Who could this be?" I asked myself, since I was not expecting anyone. As I opened the door, a man in a dark blue suit with a smiling face greeted me.

"Good morning Mr. Gubatan."

"Good morning," I responded.

"I am from John Hancock Insurance Company, your uncle sent me over."

"Is that so, why?" I inquired.

"Well, he thought that since you just got married, perhaps I can help you plan your financial future."

"That's so kind of him. Unfortunately, I must tell you that I have no future in this country."

"I'm so sorry, why is that?"

"Yesterday, I just got a letter of deportation from the immigrations department," I sadly informed him.

"Really! Fortunately, I believe I can help you with your situation."

"You must be kidding me!" I exclaimed.

"I'm serious. I can explain this to you inside."

"Well, then come in, please come in," I replied with great anticipation.

We both settled in the living room sofa facing each other. He pulled his business card, wrote something in the back, and handed it to me.

"Call this person," he said. "He is a respected former immigration officer. He just retired from the INS and has just opened his own private office. As your attorney, I am sure he can be of assistance to you."

I could hardly believe his words. I never thought of hiring an attorney . . . and a former INS officer at that!

"Don't worry about the cost; he will work with you in this regard. He just wants to help people," my visitor assured me.

"You are a godsend!" I exclaimed. "Sorry. I am not in a position to do any business with you at this time. Perhaps in the future. I've got your card anyway, and I will contact you when I am ready," I politely explained.

"Sure, Mr. Gubatan; I'm glad I was able to help. Best of luck to you," he shook my hands, and said goodbye.

As the insurance salesman left the house, I wondered if he could be an angel sent by God to direct my path. After his visit, I called my "uncle" inquiring about my visitor. With equal amazement, he said that he does not know this man from John Hancock.

> "All God's angels come to us dis-
> guised." —James Lowell

The next day, I called the recommended attorney in haste, to make an appointment. His eagerness to help me buoyed me up. I went downtown to see him in his office. As expected, he was a courteous and affable person. I explained my situation, and he told me that he was confident that he could help me. To my delight, he indicated that my case was very common.

Then we talked about financing. He simply asked me how much I could afford to pay each month. I told him, and he accepted my offer. He made me sign some papers and he advised me, "From now on, don't worry about your case; I will take care of the deportation letter. If you receive any correspondence from the INS, simply mail it to me. However, expect a court hearing before a judge in the future. Have a great day."

The Chaperon Summoned

*A*s I left his office, I could hardly wait to tell Perla what happened. I felt like a homing pigeon released to bring home some great news. A sense of newfound freedom was pulsating in my veins. Most of all, I felt like the hand of God was gently leading me to greener pastures. "How could I ever repay this awesome God? Is there no end to His goodness?" I mused. I drove home somewhat oblivious of the traffic and the crowded streets of San Francisco. For some reason the sun seem to shine a little brighter.

> "He is a man of sense who does not grieve for what he has not, but rejoices in what he has." —Epictetus

Arriving at the apartment, I found Perla saying her afternoon prayers. For me, she was like a prayer warrior, preparing for battle by committing everything to God. I sat on the living room sofa, spiritually joining her in prayer and at the same time pondering the mysterious happenings during the day. When she finished, I broke the good news to her

"We found a good lawyer, one who knows the workings of the immigrations department! I still believe that he is a Godsend."

"Really, that's great! How much did he charge you?" Perla inquired with some trepidation.

"Not much. We agreed on a reasonable monthly fee based on what we could afford. He knew I was going to school at night and that I could barely make ends meet. I tell you, that man has a kind and understanding heart."

"What else did he tell you?" Perla prodded me to say more.

"Well, he also asked me to give him any correspondence I receive from the INS."

"Is that all? How about a court hearing, will there be a one?" Perla inquired with some apprehension.

"Yes, he told me to expect a hearing. He said he will do his best to keep us in this country. For us, I think we should double our prayers asking God to continue to help us."

There was a moment of silence, then Perla said, "I agree, I will do this as I receive the Eucharist daily at mass. I have confidence that whatever happens, it will be for our own good."

"If I am distracted, Holy Communion helps me to become recollected. I arm myself for the day's cares and concerns by receiving the Eucharist." —St. Thomas More

---

Then Perla's eyes met mine, and we both understood that after what we have been through, it would be unlikely that the good Lord would just suddenly abandon us. As I stood up to place the attorney's contract in a safe place, a flash of uncertainty about the court hearing entered my mind. Fortunately, like an impulse, I simply shrugged it off.

> **"There are times in everyone's life when something constructive is born out of adversity . . . when things seem so bad that you've got to grab your faith by the shoulders and shake it."** —Anonymous

The days ahead were less stressful. I went to night school confident and determined to do better. At work, I took advantage of any opportunity to perform well. The usual mental intimidation regarding my immigrant status seem to fade away.

> **"Just keep the joy of Jesus as your strength—be happy and at peace. Accept whatever He gives; and give what- ever He takes with a big smile."**
> **—Mother Teresa of Calcutta**

But deep in my heart, I was restless. What did God want from me? Where was He leading me? Why all this roller coaster emotions and sentiments? Where will this all end?

Like a farmer who leaves the outcome of his crops to Mother Nature, and to God's divine providence, Perla and I approached our future in the same way. It has been eight months now since our wedding, and daily we would simply place all our tomorrows in the Master's hands. Occasionally I would receive some correspondence from the INS, and after reading it, I would immediately mail it to my attorney.

Then one day, another correspondence from the immigration department hit my mailbox. As usual I would immediately open the letter thinking it would be just another update; but this time it was portentous. The letter summoned us to appear before a judge at the INS Building in Sansome Street in downtown San Francisco. The date and time of the trial was carefully noted. I immediately called my attorney and informed him of the letter. He said he knew about it, and that all I needed to do was for me and Perla to appear at court. Then, he casually added, that he would do his best to win our case, although he made no promises of the outcome.

Once again, unconsciously, I succumbed to some apprehension. I told Perla about the court hearing and she too just fell silent. In retrospect, I knew this was a test of faith. The truth was, Perla's faith was stronger than mine. She went to church daily, while I went to mass only on Sundays. Pretending to be strong, I told her to remember what the good Lord told me before, "I will take care of your problem." As I uttered those words, there was a sudden burst of hope in my soul, a wonderful feeling of peace once again came over me. Somehow this change of attitude affected Perla in a positive way, and she too began to relax and simply said, "It's time for me to go to church." She left the apartment and walked over to St. Philip's church, which was only half a block away.

"Souls who do not have the habit of prayer are like paralyzed bodies with hands and feet they cannot use. It seems to me that to stop praying is to take a wrong turn, because prayer is the door through which all God's graces come to us. If this door is closed, I do not know what might happen." —St. Teresa of Avila

The Chaperon Stays

*A*t the appointed time, we traveled to the INS building located in downtown San Francisco and showed up at the courthouse. My attorney was there to greet us and simply told us to answer any questions from the judge or the prosecuting attorney.

Very shortly, the judge showed up and sat on his bench. The proceedings started with the prosecuting attorney reading the charges against us and his recommendation for immediate deportation. Everything he said was true, so I simply hung my head in silence. Then I heard the voice of the judge speak to me. "Mr. Gubatan, do you have anything to say?" Composing myself, and facing the judge I calmly and haltingly replied:

"Yes, your honor. No doubt, everything said here today is true. I do accept that I have broken the law, but without malice. I did not intentionally challenge the law, nor the government of this God loving country, but rather, I was forced by circumstances and personal financial difficulties to act as I did. Also, my desire to bring my fiancée to this land of opportunity forced my hand to do what I did. I wanted to begin a new life in this country where there is freedom and opportunity to live my life to the fullest. Your honor, if I may, I simply would like to ask for your consideration and kindness for a second chance. This country has been known for leniency to needy and desperate immigrants. Please give us that chance to begin a new life here."

There was silence. I was amazed about the words that came out of my mouth. The truth is, I did not anticipate that I would be given the chance to say anything to the judge. It was all spontaneous—perhaps orchestrated by a higher power.

> "By learning to contact, listen to,
> and act on our intuition, we can
> directly connect to the higher power
> of the universe and allow it to become
> our guiding force." —Shakti Gawain

Then the judge glanced at Perla and said, "How about you, Mrs. Gubatan? Do you have anything to say?"

I do not exactly recall what Perla said to the judge. It was more in the same line of thought as what I just expressed. She too was apologetic, and hammered the point of our helplessness and the need for a second chance. But her words, like the words of a mother, were penetrating. After she spoke there was silence in the court.

Then the judge glanced at my attorney, who stood up and spoke a few words. He mentioned the fact that Perla was pregnant and big with child, as evidenced by her large protruding tummy. He then requested the judge to extend our stay until at least the baby was safely born. The judge called both attorneys to caucus with him. After some time, the judge made some pronouncements which was hard for me to understand. Then he banged his gabble and dismissed the court.

Outside the INS building, my attorney finally explained to me what happened and what the verdict was. He said that the judge allowed our extended stay until the baby was born. Smiling, he said:

"Congratulations! Make sure the baby is delivered safely. Your child is your gateway to citizenship. After the baby is born as a US citizen, we can immediately apply for your permanent residence in this country and subsequently we can apply for your citizenship. Everything will be alright. Have a great day."

Perla and I did not know what to say, we were so overjoyed. Abruptly, we managed to utter, "Thank you. Thank very much." At the same time, imperceptibly, I said, "Thank you Lord!"

"When asked if my cup is half-full or half-empty my only response is that I am thankful I have a cup." —Sam Lefkowitz

Driving home that morning, Perla and I were silent. We were just overwhelmed by the positive outcome of our case. Not only will our first-born child be a magnificent gift from God, but would also be our bridge to citizenship. I thought to myself, "How's that for hitting two birds with one stone?"

"We are told that talent creates its own opportunities. But it sometimes seems that intense desire creates not only its own opportunities, but its own talents." —Eric Hoffer

---

The traffic going home was heavy, but somehow it didn't bother me. I was pondering these questions: What does this all mean? What is God saying to me? What does God want?

When we arrived home, Perla did her usual chores with palpable equanimity. I had previously notified my employer about my one day absence, so I had the rest of the day off. My mind was still savoring the favorable court decision, and my heart was singing. As evening drew near, my adulation was mounting like a volcano showing signs of eruption. I was unsure of how to release this potential energy of appreciation and gratitude. Simultaneously, I had this nagging question again, "What does God want from me?"

That night after I said my usual prayers, I hit the sack hoping to doze off immediately. But the unexplained "spiritual volcanic energy" was percolating in my consciousness, I could not sleep. Perla who was next to me was already in dreamland. I continued to toss back and forth. "Why can't I fall asleep?" I murmured. I glanced at the clock, it was midnight! Then gently, from out of the blue, a thought hit me, "Might as well spend this time in prayer." I slid off the bed, fell on my knees, and bowed my head. I felt the "mystical volcanic spiritual energy" surging in my chest. Instinctively, I closed my eyes and prayed in earnest:

"O God, Lord Jesus, you have once again surprised me. I was expecting a long court battle . . . but here it is, the storm has subsided. I know you engineered this for Perla and myself; you were the hands that moved the players in the courthouse. How can I repay you? I have nothing much to offer you, I am but a poor creature."

87

The "mystical volcanic spiritual energy" within me surged even stronger. I was now breathing in a much slower pace. I did not fully understand what was going on. I could only feel a warm pulsating sensation in my body. I reached deeper into my soul, and this time I affectionately uttered:

"Lord Jesus, you know I fully appreciate what you did on the cross for my redemption. I told you this last time. But now, even though I have never said this before . . . I dare to say it now. I love you! I love you Lord Jesus! I love you, and I give my heart to you. It is all yours!"

I meant everything I said, every single word that erupted from my heart. Like a gentle summer rain or a warm sacramental oil cascading down my head, this warm soothing sensation traveled across my whole body. I began to tremble. Tears fell like the dewfall from heaven down my cheeks. I felt covered with a gentle, mystical, esoteric kind of love. At that moment, I wanted to die of inner joy. I wanted the Lord's mystical loving embrace to last forever. Why? Because it was the greatest flowering in my soul, ever.

"The interior life is like a sea of love in which the soul is plunged and is, as it were, drowned in love. —St. John Vianney

In a moment of clarity, I wanted profusely to thank God. "How can I reciprocate this love?" I thought. Then in a burst of total transparency and honesty, I said without calculating the cost:

"Lord, in gratitude for what you have done, I promise to go to mass every day. The rest of my days, I will worship you by receiving Holy Communion daily."

After I said this, I felt that I have done my part, that I have given my best. Feeling peaceful and content, moments later, I went back to bed and fell asleep like a baby with a smile in my face.

"Give thanks for sorrow that teaches you compassion; for pain that teaches you courage . . . and give exceeding thanks for the mystery which remains a mystery still; the veil that hides you from the infinite, which makes it possible for you to believe in what you cannot see." —Robert Nathan

The next day, I felt like a carefree bird, chirping and hopping about, ready to fly to the limits of life's horizon. With excitement, I told Perla I would go to the afternoon mass after work. Since I never went to weekday masses, she was befuddled. I just smiled and kissed her goodbye as I headed for work. Thus began my daily attendance at mass. I was surprised to have kept this promise despite the challenges of weather, traffic, and unforeseen peaks and valleys at work. It became a habit and a top priority. It is hard to mention all the many blessings I have received from this single commitment, it has literally changed my life.

As I went to daily mass to receive the Eucharist, I felt it as a source of inner strength and joy. The Eucharist was so special that it was for me the highlight of the day. It made the challenges I faced at work appear surmountable and not as burdensome. At this stage of my "love walk" with the good Lord, I felt like living an "enchanted life." The truth is, I never imagined that there could be such a blissful state of life. Perhaps some would refer to this as the "spiritual honeymoon" stage. Will it be like this every day?

Looking back, it appears that the hand of God was re-arranging the pieces of my life like the chairs of the Titanic which were drastically re-arranged during its sinking. There were so many changes for me.

I was in Manila over a year ago, now I find myself in San Francisco. I was single then, now I am happily married. I was on a student visa then, now I was on track to be an American citizen. Most significant for me was the spiritual change I experienced. From a mediocre love of God to a stronger commitment to Him. From a lukewarm affection, to an enthusiastic abiding in Him. From a shallow relationship, to a robust connection with His desires. As if in one swoop, I have somewhat scaled Mount Moriah, the mountain of sacrifice. Now based on this draconian changes in my life, I clearly saw the hand of God. When we feel and have a sense of the presence of God in our lives, we are filled with tremendous joy.

At this point, as I look back, the chaperon days were like a sweet aroma of a beckoning. Beckoning to pure love, beckoning to spiritual love, beckoning to a personal relationship with God. Yes, those were "enchanted" days, never to be forgotten, simply because they were ordained by the greatest lover of all, the Son of God.

As the writer of Psalm 139 declare, "Where can I go from your spirit, from your presence where can I flee? If I go to the heavens you are there, if I sink to the nether world you are present there. If I take the wings of the dawn, if I settle at the farthest limits of the sea, even there your hand shall guide me, and your right hand hold me fast."

Is God writing the story of my life? Most of the time I think so. When I utter the words; "Master, let your most holy will and your Divine Providence be accomplished in my life," I can sense His pen inscribing something about me in the book of life." I think that He too will write the story of your life if you let Him.

The Bread of Life

*W*hy are some people attracted to Jesus, while others are not? Of the six billion people on earth, only around two billion has some faith and belief in the Son of God. Why? I'm not sure, but for me, it remains a paradox and an enigma.

Sundar Singh who was a new Hindu convert to Christianity was distributing copies of the Gospel of John to passengers in a train headed for Mumbai, India. One passenger took a copy of the Gospel and tore it to pieces, then in anger threw them out of the window. That seem to be the end of the episode. However, Divine Providence chose to involve a man named Ananda.

He was walking along the railroad tracks when he happened to pick up a small piece of paper and read the words, which were written in his native language, with curiosity. It simply read, "the bread of life." He had no idea what it meant, so he inquired among his friends. He was told that the words were from a Christian book. However, he was advised not to read the book because it would defile him.

But Ananda was fascinated by the words, "the bread of life." He purposely decided to buy a copy of the New Testament in a bookstore. The clerk showed him the phrase where Jesus said, "I am the bread of life. Whoever comes to me will never be hungry, and whoever believes in me will never be thirsty." Ananda was intrigued and spellbound by the words of Jesus. As a result, he eagerly studied the Gospel of John, was attracted to Jesus, and later had a conversion experience. To everyone's surprise, Ananda ended up becoming a preacher.

This brings us to the question why others are not attracted to Jesus. Consider the words of Jesus, "No one can come to me unless the Father who sent me draw him." Essentially, the root of the fascination and attraction to Jesus is that it is a gift; a precious gift from the Father. That's why even among Christian families, not all are attracted to Jesus. In my own family lineage, there are Catholics, Protestants, agnostics, atheist, and even Buddhist. Indeed, how true are the words of Jesus at the last supper, "Father all those you gave me, I would have in my company." Clearly then, you and I were given by the Father to Jesus; that's why we recognize Jesus, the Son of God, as our Lord and Savior.

As a parallel, it is noteworthy to discern that those who are attracted to Jesus are also attracted to the "bread of life." Why? Because Jesus is our bread of life.

He said so in John 6:32 and onward. He said the following beautiful and inspiring words of hope:

*** "I am telling you the truth, what Moses gave you was not the bread from heaven. It is my Father who gives you the real bread from heaven. For the bread that God gives is he who comes down from heaven and gives life to the world."

*** "I am the bread of life. He who come to me will never be hungry; he who believes in me will never be thirsty. Everyone whom my Father gives me, will come to me. I will never turn away anyone who comes to me, because I have come down from heaven to do not my own will, but the will of him who sent me. For what the Father wants is that all who see the Son and believe in him should have eternal life. And I will raise them to life on the last day."

*** "I am the living bread that came down from heaven. If anyone eats this bread, he will live forever. The bread that I will give him is my flesh which I give so that the world may live. I am telling you the truth; if you do not eat the flesh of the Son of Man and drink his blood, you will not have life in you."

*** "For my flesh is the real food, my blood is the real drink. Whoever eats my flesh and drinks my blood lives in me, and I will live in him."

These are powerful, life-giving words of Jesus. He speaks about Holy Communion as we know it in the Church. Receiving Jesus' body and blood in the Eucharist gives us strength, hope and inner joy. In addition, it can transform our hearts and bring dignity to our lives. No wonder Jesus intentionally instituted the Eucharist, or Holy Communion, because he wanted to make sure we have all the spiritual sustenance and provisions we need for our journey to the Messianic Banquet. That's why St. Augustine said, "God is all to you: if you are hungry, he is bread; if thirsty he is water; if darkness, he is light; if naked, he is a robe of immortality." The Eucharist then, is the source and summit of our faith, because it is Jesus himself who comes to us and inhabit our very souls. This brings us perfect joy.

The Talent

*W*arren Buffet is regarded as the guru of investors. Today he has a net worth of about 62 billion dollars and is sought by high ranking officials for his economic advice. Although an agnostic, his economic principles are in line with Gospel precepts. He is known for not carrying a cell phone or having a computer in his desk. He thinks independently and avoids being influenced by Wall Street or any popular financial trends. In short, he has his own approach to investment.

Buffet's first principle is: Don't bury your money. Don't hide it under a pillow. Instead invest it, trade it, or deposit it in a bank to gain interest. Don't let it sit idle. Does this sound familiar?

In one of Jesus' parables, the Master of the house severely scolded his servant who buried the one talent (one gold coin) he was given. However, the other servants who invested the talents entrusted to them were highly praised and rewarded by the Master. Why? Because the Master expected something in return. In the business world, we would call this ROI, or return on investment. The Master expected the servants to put to good use the talents given to them and grow it.

Most people today are born with natural gifts or God-given talents. Some are born with artistic abilities, good looks, or intelligence; like Buffet who was born with a knack for numbers and business. Others are born with deep faith, compassion, and charity. Like Mother Teresa of Calcutta who was a spiritual genius who saw Jesus in the poorest of the poor. What if Mother Teresa did not use her gift of compassion and deep faith? Then the poor, the lepers, the orphans of India would not have experienced God's love and comfort in the person of Mother Teresa. Perhaps the greatest tragedy would be for someone to face the Master at the end of life and give an account of his God-given gifts or talents by saying, "I did nothing with the talents you gave me; I did not put it to good use."

Buffet's second principle is: When you invest in something, look at its intrinsic value, not its market value. In other words, don't invest in a company based on the stock market price. Instead research the true value of the company by knowing its product, its management, its workers, and its ethics. Know the company well in and out. Then make your investment decision. In the same way, Jesus' teachings and parables boils down to knowing and assessing the intrinsic value of a person.

Remember the story of the woman caught in adultery; the crowd was ready to stone her because they saw no value in her because she was a sinner. But Jesus saw something in her which the crowd did not see. He saw her infinite worth. He saw the great potential of a redeemed and transformed sinner. In the end, Jesus would invest his entire life and his sacrifice on the cross for poor sinners. He would intentionally invest his whole life for you and for me.

Buffet's third principle is: Be charitable and help others who are in need. His many charitable foundations are well known among philanthropists. In fact, he was credited for having made the largest charitable donation in history in the amount of thirty billion dollars. An article about this described him as follows:

"Despite his wealth, Buffet does not measure success by dollars. In 2006, he pledged to give away almost his entire fortune to charities, primarily the Bill and Melinda Gates Foundation. He's adamant about not funding monuments to himself; no Warren Buffet buildings or halls. He says, 'I know people who have a lot of money, and they get testimonial dinners and hospital wings named after them. But the truth is that nobody in the world loves them. When you get to my age, you'll measure your success in life by how many of the people you want to love you actually do love you. That's the ultimate test of how you've lived your life." For me, I would like to add my own simple investment principles.

First, invest in meaningful relationships. Why? Because it will sustain you in good times and in bad times. Foremost, invest in your relationship with God. Give it attention and significance. Avoid any kind of ho-hum, luke-warm, mediocre, and shallow relationship with Him. Instead invest in a sincere and intense relationship with God. With this kind of deep and meaningful relationship, then it would be easier to invest in your relationship with your family, friends, co-workers, and neigh-bors. When you do this, happiness is just around the corner.

Second, invest in good works and spiritual works of mercy. Have some kind of ministry to the poor, the sick, and the elderly. Also, consider a ministry to bring young people to a knowledge and love of God. Doing this you will develop a sense of wholeness and peace.

Thirdly, invest in daily prayer and worship. Without prayers, we are like nomads roaming in the desert without any sense of direction. Without prayers, we are helpless and hopeless in facing the world of vanity, violence, and vitriol. But with prayers, we are animated by the spirit of goodness, beauty and truth. With prayers, we are embraced in God's love and presence. With prayers, we can experience inner peace and joy.

The Main Thing

A preacher once said, "The main thing is to keep the main thing, the main thing." Naturally, we wonder what this main thing really is. Based on our personal experience and background, each person would have his own idea.

Fr. John Powell, a Philosophy Professor at Loyola University in Chicago tells the story of Tommy. Tommy was the agnostic rebel in his class. However, during the final exam, as he handed his papers to Fr. John, he said, "Will I ever find God?" The priest replied, "No, I think God will find you." Months later, Tommy graduated but kept in touch with Fr. John.

One beautiful morning, Tommy paid Fr. John a visit and told him that he was diagnosed with terminal cancer. Haltingly he said, "Father I still remember what you said, that God will find me. I'm ready, and I want to be at the right place when God looks for me. What do you suggest?"

The priest looked at Tommy with affection and said, "You can start by telling those you care about that you love them."

Tommy took the advice seriously and started with his mother. This was easy since his mother was a caring person. When his mother was fixing her bed, Tommy approached her and said, "Mother I just wanted to tell you that I appreciate your putting up with me and that I love you."

Her mother stopped what she was doing, embraced Tommy as only a mother can and said with teary eyes, "I love you too, Tommy. You know I love you."

Now, Tommy's dad was a hard case. They had argued many times before, and they were not in good terms. But Tommy made up his mind. While his dad was reading the newspaper in the living room, Tommy slowly approached him and uttered, "Dad, can we talk?" Immediately, his dad replied, "About what?" without lowering the newspaper. Gingerly, Tommy uttered, "I just want to tell you that I'm sorry for giving you a hard time."

The newspaper slowly went down. Sensing an opportunity, Tommy continued, "I also wanted to let you know that I love you. I love you dad." The newspaper fell to the floor. Then his dad for the first time in many years embraced Tommy. Both their eyes were moist with tears.

His dad finally whispered, "I love you too Tommy. I love you."

As days went by, Tommy continued to make every effort to tell his friends and those who visited him, that he loved them. Subsequently, he called Fr. John and informed him, "You were right, Father. I followed your advice, and God found me. And I found him too. I know he has forgiven me, I know he loves me. And you know what? I love him too."

A few day later, Fr. John was notified that Tommy died. For the priest, it was an unforgettable experience of God's personal love and care for his people; most of all, for his infinite mercy to all who seek him. God will find you! He is always seeking you! *This is the main thing, to open our hearts and allow God to find us. Why? Because therein lies pure joy.*

Spiritual Awakening

Once in a lifetime, people experience something that will change their lives forever. It actually comes after a series of setbacks, followed by small victories. As they string these small victories together, they begin to see a pattern that touches their hearts and souls. These cumulative positive changes can result in an uplifting spiritual awakening. Take the case of Mike Gill, who wrote the book *How Starbucks Saved My Life*. Here's his story.

He was born into luxury and graduated from Yale University. Unfortunately, Mike was unfaithful to his wife and disgraced his four children. He had an affair with a psychiatrist and had a son by her. Later she left him, and the next thing Mike knew, he was fired from his job. Since he had squandered his money and was now sixty-four years old, he started looking for work.

One morning, he went to Starbucks for a cup of coffee. Crystal, the young manager thought he was looking for work, and since it was hiring week, she offered Mike a job. He took the job and began to learn the intricacies of making an array of different specialty coffee and serving them to ordinary people. He also learned the Starbucks' philosophy that every customer is called a Guest, and that every employee is a Partner. With this in mind, every Guest and every Partner must be treated with respect and dignity. This was quite a revelation for Mike.

Along this line, he also learned employees must make eye contact and conversation with every customer. After some time, Mike got to know the customers by name, which they in turn fondly called him Mike. Soon he began to value precious moments of truly human interaction. For him this was a major switch in attitude towards other people. As a consequence, he realized that serving people was not a job, but a way of life. However, the most important thing Mike found out was a new meaning in life, which gave him a new source of joy.

In addition, he also learned the importance of recognition and appreciation. Why? Because at Starbucks they were trained to recognize unselfish good works. They were trained to catch people doing good and appreciate them—rather than catch them making unintentional mistakes. Either way, Mike felt good when he appreciated others, and when he was recognized for a job well done.

For Mike, this new experience was like a beautiful spiritual awakening. He wrote, "Crystal and my Partners at Starbucks had given me a chance to work, and live, and see things in a new way. I had been a control freak. I had loved ordering people to work overtime, or change a headline, or even bring me a cup of coffee. I had been a really bad boss. It was time to be a really good Partner. I had traded my pin-striped suit for a green apron, a Master of the Universe costume for something that said: 'I was there to serve, not to rule.'"

Mike's brand new spiritual experience eventually reconciled him with his wife and children. They were truly amazed to see him serving coffee to street people, enjoying it while affectionately greeted everyone. Most of all they were astounded by his happiness. This wholesome image renewed their love and respect for the "old man." What can we glean from Mike's spiritual adventure?

First, we must realize that what really matters is a healthy and faithful relationship with God, family, and neighbor. This can be achieved by treating everyone with respect and dignity.

Second, we can recognize and appreciate the good things other people do. Try to catch them doing good, and then tell them right away. Don't wait till the next day.

Third, learn that life is not about controlling people, but about giving them opportunity for human interaction, so that in the process we can determine ways to be of service to them. As Mike would often say, "I was there to serve, not to rule." In conclusion, let us therefore be grateful for "second chances" in life, so we can serve and appreciate others, be the best person we can be, and do it all for the honor and glory of God. Doing this brings us inner peace and joy.

The Presence

*F*or a moment, take this time to ponder upon a Master-Disciple dialogue captured below:

"Master," said the disciple, "I saw a man who could fly."

"So?" said the Master, "a bird can fly."

"Master," said the disciple, "I saw a man who could live under water."

"So?" said the Master, "a fish can live under water."

"Master," said the disciple, "I saw a man who in the twinkling of an eye, could move from one town to another."

"So?" said the Master, "Satan can do that."

"If you wish to find something truly extraordinary," the Master continued, "find a man who can be present to people and keep his thoughts on God."

Why is the last criterion so important? Because this is the secret of Mother Teresa of Calcutta. She has been known to be fully present to people even during conversation, while at the same time being conscious of God. You can sense that she is very much in touch with God even though she is fully engaged in conversing with you. And if you asked her why this is important, she will simply say, "So you can see the Christ in others, especially among the poor."

One time Mother Teresa was invited by the Bishop of Cuba to open a house for the poor in Havana. In the process, she was asked to visit Cuba and talk to Fidel Castro. Always humble and unpretentious, the conversation with Castro went like this:

Castro, "Let's see, Mother, what is the work which your Sisters propose to do in Cuba?"

Mother Teresa, "The Sisters are coming to work for the poorest of the poor."

Castro, "Well, here, after the Revolution, the class of poor people no longer exists. Here, thanks to the Revolution, everyone has work and all Cubans have their basic necessities taken care of. Our healthcare and educational systems figure among the best in the world."

Mother Teresa, "Very fine, Mister President. But are there not people here who find themselves alone, children abandoned by their parents, single mothers and their children abandoned, old people neglected by their families, alcoholics, here where they have so much rum? Are there not former prisoners here who have no place to go when they get out of jail?"

Castro, "Are you telling me, Mother, that you and your sisters bother with these types of people?"

Mother Teresa, "Yes, Mister President. These people are also children of God. Yes, we work for them."

Castro, "Ah, well then. Come, Mother. The Revolution and the Cuban people welcome you."

What a gift! Mother Teresa with her gift of presence and her gift of bringing God's presence to others, can open the door of charity even in the heart of a communist leader. Presence, presence, presence. Presence to God and presence to others, this is indeed a priceless gift.

No wonder St. Ignatius Loyola said, "He who remembers the presence of God is less open to other thoughts, especially bad thoughts. As long as we believe that God sees us, we are restrained from daring to sin before such a Witness and Judge. In two ways, the presence of God is an antidote against sin: first because God sees us, and second, because we see God."

What a spiritual gem, to be conscious of the Lord's presence in all that we say and do.

The Unexamined Life

$\mathcal{M}$ost New Year's days connote new opportunities and new beginnings. It is also a good time to let go of the stigma of the past year and start with a fresh examination of the direction of your life. As Plato said, "The unexamined life is not worth living." However, for Christians, this examination is centered in our relationship with others and with our God.

Relationship with God is either shallow or deep, mediocre or outstanding, humdrum or profound, personal or superficial. In the Book of Revelation, God warns the church of Laodicea:

"I know your deeds; I know you are neither hot nor cold. How I wish you were one or the other—hot or cold. But because you are lukewarm, neither hot nor cold, I will spit you out of my mouth. You keep saying, "I am so rich and secure that I want for nothing." Little do you realize how wretched you are, how pitiable and poor, how blind and naked!" (Rev. 3:16)

Obviously, the culprit, the demise, the downfall is lukewarm-ness. God hates luke-warm-ness. That's why God says, "I will spit you out of my mouth." What an indictment. We are cast out from his presence. Just like if you ask someone you love so profoundly and so dearly, "Do you love me?" And he/she says, "I don't know, I am so busy. I really don't care."

Wow!!! What a slap in the face. What a spit in the face. Having a lukewarm love of God is unacceptable and shameful.

On one occasion, after a church service, someone came to me asking for prayer for a successful neck surgery. She said the surgery was somewhat complicated. We talked a little bit more. Without my asking her, she confided to me that one of my homilies about the nature of love has changed her outlook in life. She said:

"I used to be very casual and lukewarm about Jesus. The mass, the Eucharist did not mean much to me. I had a humdrum and shallow relationship with God. Interiorly, I was not happy and secure. I had that sickening fear of the future, and I was restless. Now I am no longer lukewarm with God, thanks to your admonition. Now I am seriously attracted and attached in a loving way to Jesus. I affectionately think of him most of the time. So I have lovingly surrendered this coming surgery to him. I am at peace, but I still need prayers." Before we parted, we prayed together.

Therefore, let us examine our connection and bonding with the Lord. Let us focus on deepening our unique loving partnership with the God of the universe. No more lukewarm and mediocre love of the Lord. After all, he made us for himself, he made us for intimacy, he made us for heaven. Pursuing this goal will bring us inner peace and joy.

Cost of Discipleship

To be a disciple of Jesus is risky and can be unconventional. Many are called, but few volunteer. Why? Because most people want safety, prestige, and a big paycheck.

This reminds me of what a volunteer in 1983 was asked before he could join the Sanctuary Movement here in the USA. The Sanctuary Movement comprised of various Christian congregations trying to help persecuted refugees from Central America, like El Salvador and Nicaragua. Military Dictators at the time were ruthless and merciless. One time a volunteer was interviewed.

"Before you say whether you really wish to join us, let me ask you some questions."

"Are you ready to have your telephone tapped by the government?

"Are you prepared to have your neighbors shun you?"

"Are you strong enough to have your children ridiculed and harassed at school?"

"And are you ready to be arrested and tried, with full media coverage?"

"If you are not prepared for these things, you may not be ready to join the movement. Because when push comes to shove, if you fear these things, you will not be ready to do what needs to be done for the refugees."

The volunteer decided to think it over. The cost of discipleship was just too much for him.

Then I remembered Dietrich Bonhoeffer, the German theologian who was executed by the Nazis in 1945 for his resisting the slaughter of Jews. He wrote the book *The Cost of Discipleship*, which called for a radical obedience to Christ and a rebuke of comfortable Christianity. He was the one who coined the word cheap grace. He said:

"Cheap grace is preceding forgiveness without requiring repentance, baptism without church discipline, communion without confession. Cheap grace, the mortal enemy of our church, is grace without discipleship, grace without a commitment to Christ."

Obviously, Bonhoeffer understood the sacrificial nature of grace, which reflect the sacrificial nature of loving God. Why? Because God must come first, no matter what. Jesus must be our first and last love. To bring home the point let me tell you of one man's search for true love.

When he was a young lad, Pope Francis played soccer, loved to dance the tango, and later began to work as an apprentice in a food chemistry lab. At the age of seventeen, he had developed a new set of friends associated with the Catholic Action group. One very close friend who was also active in the Catholic Action group attracted him so much that he planned to propose marriage to her during a picnic arranged by his friends. For the group, Francis' engagement was apparent.

So, on a gorgeous summer day on his way to the picnic, he happened to pass by his parish church. He felt a mysterious tug to make a visit. Inside the church he met a holy priest whom he has never seen before. Francis was so attracted to the spirituality of the priest that he requested the priest to hear his confession. And there it happened, at the confessional, he heard the call of God for him to become a priest. Without hesitation, he said "Yes." And here's what Pope Francis said about the experience.

"During that confession something unusual happened to me. I cannot say what, but it was something that changed my life. I would say that it was as though I had been surprised, while my guard was down. It was the surprise, the amazement of an encounter for which I realized I had been waiting. God became for me the One who goes ahead of you. You are seeking Him, and He seeks you first. You want to meet Him, but He comes to meet you first."

In the end, Francis never made it to the picnic. He seemed to have left all of that behind. Was this peak religious experience a kind of divine intervention? Did this encounter give him a "new heart" and a new purpose in life? He answered the call to discipleship, and he found tremendous inner peace and joy. Obviously, to answer God's call is the door to a lifetime of purpose and meaning, culminating in some kind of union with God.

Creative Waiting

*I*n the ceiling above the altar of the Sistine Chapel in the Vatican is the magnificent painting of Michelangelo depicting the last judgment and the second coming of Christ. It portrayed myriads of souls ascending into heaven while others were descending into purgatory or hell. Despite the ingenious composition of the artwork, Cardinal Carafa and his friend Biago de Cesena complained to Pope Julius II about the painting because it depicted nude figures of men and women representing human souls.

The great Michelangelo got annoyed at Biago for complaining to the Pope so he purposely painted his face with his naked soul in hell. With a stroke of genius Michelangelo also placed Biago's face and naked figure just above the entrance door of the chapel so everyone would notice it. Greatly embarrassed, Biago appealed to the Pope for this face to be erased from the painting. Silently the Pope pondered the request then said, "My jurisdiction does not extend to hell, so what Michelangelo has painted, it shall remain." If you happen to visit the Sistine Chapel, look for the face of Biago de Cesena in the chapel entrance.

Since no one knows when the second coming of Christ as depicted in Michelangelo's fresco will happen except God the Father, what do we do in the interim? For some who are artistically inclined, we simply engage in creative waiting. But what is it? Perhaps it is best to describe it as a metaphor.

It is like a trapeze artist who lets go of the swinging bar he is clinging to so tightly, and after letting it go, waits there in mid-air for the other bar to come from the other side and give him a new lifeline. This is often called the mid-air transition. It can be scary. It can be temporary, or it can be a quick transition to the next life. As always you hope for the best.

In 1995, I had this temporary mid-air transition. At the time, I was faced with two big dilemmas. First, I was notified by my employer of a factory closure due to lack of business. Second, I was suddenly diagnosed after a simple annual physical exam, of a serious ailment that could be terminal. At this point I felt disoriented. Psychologically, it was overwhelming because of the intensity of the

problems. It was obvious that my life was
"on hold."

In this state of bewilderment, I noticed
that I was not my usual self. Sometimes I
ate too little, and sometimes I ate too much.
Sometimes I was silent when I should talk,
and sometimes I would talk too much when I
should be silent. At times, I tried to hide my
fears, and at times, I would overstate it. In
a peculiar way, I would start things which I
did not intend to finish, or at times finished
things which someone else started. Puzzling at
times, I would get tired of friends inquiring
about my health, and at other times, felt
hurt when they didn't ask. I was a mix bag of
"chips and crackers." But there were moments
of great light. By the grace of God, I had
some insights of how to cope with this mid-air
transition.

First, I realized that I was more than
what was happening to me, or the gargantuan
problems I was facing. I discovered I had
spiritual roots deeper than my consciousness.
These roots were divine grounding based on
an intimate knowledge and relationship with
the all-powerful and loving God. This experience of the transcendent pointed me to the
reality that:

❖ It is astonishing to know that we never feel alone when we are in love with the Son of God.

❖ Prayer moves the hand that moves the world.

❖ Love is a miracle because it is always willing to do the impossible, and for God, nothing is impossible.

❖ Love unlocks doors that were not even there before.

❖ Sometimes we seek answers to our prayers more than we seek the One who answers them, Jesus the Lord.

Considering all of the above, it is clear that this creative waiting is fruitful when we are grounded in the truth of God's never ending love. In my case, it has proven all of the above Christian maxims to be absolutely true. In the end, I survived both dilemmas and made me a confident, happier, and hopeful person. It has changed my life and perspective forever.

The Object of My Love

$\mathcal{L}$ooking for champions of our faith, we often look up to saints like Peter and Paul. After all, both of them were martyred when they gave up their lives as powerful witnesses of the Gospel. As a testimonial of their fidelity to Jesus, you can visit the eternal city of Rome, and there you will find the magnificent and separate basilicas dedicated to St. Peter and St. Paul.

Of course, they did not become saints overnight. Like us, they too struggled with the idea of being totally dedicated to following Jesus. Sometimes they would get things right and sometimes getting things wrong.

Like Peter, he fell asleep while Jesus was praying and agonizing in the Garden of Gethsemane; although he was told by Jesus to stay awake and pray. There are times however, when Peter gets it right; like when he boldly proclaimed in front of the disciples that Jesus is the Messiah and the Son of God. Of course, this enlightenment came from the Father.

The same is true with Paul; he too did not get it right the first time. In fact, he was so busy persecuting the early Christians in Rome that God had to knock him off his horse on his way to Damascus to get his attention and get him on the right track. Obviously, both Peter and Paul struggled to get things right. However, in the end, realizing the object of their love, they gave their lives following Jesus. In the process, they became champions of God's love.

Sometimes we get it right, and sometimes we don't. However, this does not mean that we don't love Jesus or preclude us from striving hard to be a faithful follower of Him. Remember, it is in our missing the point, then getting the point, that we begin to know the patience, mercy and love of God. When we realize this goodness of God, we slowly fall in love with him. Note the beautiful saying: Trip over love and you can get up, but fall in love with God, and you fall forever.

There are times when I get the Peter and Paul syndrome. Sometimes my head gets it, but then my heart gets distracted and seduced by the world when things get tough. As a result, I get mixed up and confused. However, when my heart gets it; that Jesus is the sole object of my life, and he is the true source of my happiness, then I get things right. I fall in love with Jesus again, and I find peace and happiness.

I read of a young girl of twelve, who is from the beautiful slopes of Garabandal, Spain. Her name is Conchita Gonzales. She is one of the four visionaries who had a series of apparitions of the Virgin Mary, the mother of Jesus. This personal encounter with Mary completely changed her life in 1961. Her spiritual eyes were opened, and her perception of life became lucid in light of Mary's admonitions.

One time she was interviewed by Dr. Jeronimo Dominguez at length, and I will just mention a small portion of it to bring home a point:

Doctor: The Virgin also said in the message that above all, we have to be good. What do you think she meant by that?

Conchita: I don't know what the Virgin meant. I understand it to be *a life lived moment by moment offering everything to God.* Living like a Christian, the way our conscience tells us, is what I think she meant.

Doctor: So, everyone can be good?

Conchita: Sure. Everyone in the practice of their religion . . . knows how to be good because each person has his own conscience and *God speaks to each one through their conscience.*

Doctor: What have you done or what have you tried to do to live the message?

Conchita: What would give the Virgin great happiness is a very difficult thing for me. That is to *live each moment of the day doing everything for God.*

So here is a young girl's illuminated view of getting it right. Without mentioning it, her trajectory is simply to love God. With the aid of the Virgin, she desires to live each moment for God and offer her very best to honor God. This, in her uncomplicated way, is being good. When we are good in the eyes of God, we can experience happiness and peace.

Be Happy!

Consolata Betrone was a pious Italian mystic who became a Capuchin nun in 1930. The Lord has blessed her with many visitations and on one occasion, Jesus told her, "Love me and you will be happy, the more you love me the happier you will be." This is such a jewel of an admonition. It is worth imbedding this in our hearts and in our consciousness. To love Jesus is to find happiness!!!

Could this be the secret of true happiness? Yet this principle is so overlooked and even misunderstood by many. Why? Because to love God is a personal matter. Every person has his own way of expressing his love of God. Each person has his own ability to love God, and his own capacity to love God. As a result, we all have our own notion and understanding of happiness, but the firm impact is clear: I am happier when I love God. And when I am happy, I am filled with joy.

But let's look at some other perceptions of happiness.

Anton Chekhov said, "Men are made for happiness, and anyone who is completely happy has a right to say to himself—I am doing God's will on earth."

Benjamin Franklin said, "The U.S. Constitution doesn't guarantee happiness, only the pursuit of it. You have to catch up with it yourself."

St. Augustine said, "Order your soul; reduce your wants; live in charity; associate in Christian community; obey the laws; trust in Providence."

Edward Young said, "For me, happiness came from prayer to a kindly God, faith in a kindly God, love for my fellow man, and doing the very best I could every day of my life. I looked for happiness in fast living, but it was not there. I tried to find it in money, but it was not there, either. But when I place myself in tune with what I believe, when I began to develop my limited ability, to rid my mind of all kinds of tangled thoughts and fill it with zeal and courage and love, when I gave myself a chance by treating myself decently and sensibly, I began to feel the stimulating, warm glow of happiness."

Based on the above insights, there's the combination of trust in God's will, faith in God, and loving our fellow man in our quest for happiness. These are solid principles. These are paths to true happiness. These are the truths of the Gospel.

But let me give you a final quote from Jesus. He said to the holy mystic and nun Consolata Betrone:

"My heart is divine, yes, but it is also human like yours; and it longs for your love, for your every thought. I shall take care of everything, even the most trivial matters, but you must think only of me. That soul is dearest to me, who loves me the most."

This is a win-win situation. We are most happy when we love the Lord, and He too is happy when we love him back.

Endless Love

*L*ove is essentially about commitment and willingness to sacrifice. It is about knowing that you cannot love and be selfish. That you cannot be selfish and be happy. That you cannot love and be stingy. This is the domain of love—generosity and happiness. That's why we pray, worship, and give alms. But in a deeper sense, pure love is really about abstaining from anything that hinders us from loving God intensely. Why?

Because love is not love if it is not intense.

Love is not love without a flame.

Love is not love without a commitment.

Love is a miracle because it is willing to do the impossible.

And love is so generous that it never counts the cost.

Robert was an idealistic seven-year-old boy raised as a Christian. At a young age, he learned to practice the adage that there is nothing small in the service of God, and that there is nothing so kingly as kindness.

One day, he went house to house to sell pencils so he could send the money to the poor children dying of hunger in Africa. And he did this with great enthusiasm. One home-owner asked him, "How much money do you intend to raise?"

With a smile, Robert replied, "A thousand dollars, sir."

"Do you plan to do this alone?" the home-owner inquired.

With confidence, Robert said, "No sir, I have my little cousin helping me out."

"Good luck!" the man exclaimed.

After a short pause, Robert replied, "Sir, I have good luck. I just need your contribution."

What a big and confident heart Robert has! Without knowing it, he proved that love is a miracle because it is always willing to do the impossible.

As Christians, we too are challenged to experience this "miracle of love." Perhaps to patch up a relationship that had gone sour for years by making the first move towards recon-ciliation. Perhaps to help someone in need or teach Catechism in a nearby Christian school. The possibilities of giving to experience this "miracle of love" is endless.

But there is a catch. We must understand, that to love, is to be vulnerable. This means to be totally open, abandoned, and surrendered to the One we love; Jesus, the Son of God. If we try too hard to love, then we are not vulnerable because we want to be in control. And love is not love if it wants to control. Why? Because true love always wants to love and give freely. It will not count the cost; nor will it count the reward. All it desires is the joy of loving and serving the One we love; the Lamb of God who takes away the sins of the world. To live this way is to find the fountain of happiness.

I Miss God

*U*sually after being temporarily separated from someone you love, either by time or space, there is a sense of lovesickness. And we know that at this point, love becomes stronger, and loneliness sets in.

Julian Barnes, a famous British author of the book *Nothing to Be Afraid*, said, "I don't believe in God, but I miss him." Is this a contradiction; someone who doesn't believe and even know God desiring his companionship? Is this a slip in consciousness, or is it the "loving hand of God?"

Throughout his book, Barnes ponders how to make sense of life and death even without a connection to a "life source." He is challenged by the enigma of existence and its demanding priorities of life. He is really hoping to find some kind of rest in a decent place.

Fortunately, I believe in God, and you believe in God! We can find rest. It is not that Barnes is ignorant, it is because he has not been touched by pure love. That's why we must be excited about sharing God's love with others so they too can be freed from loneliness and emptiness. Why? So they may realize how truly they are missing God. This is charity. This is pure love. Doing this will bring us happiness.

Wings of Rest

*T*here was a time many years ago when I
felt so tired and weary. I saw my world
collapsing, and in my mind, I was like going
through the eye of a needle. Who can squeeze
through this kind of dilemma?

It was a time when there was a big announce-
ment during an "all hands meeting" in the
assembly plant where I worked. We were told
that within thirty days, our factory would be
closing. Exit details will be formally mailed
to each employee.

That was sad. Even sadder was the fact that
during my annual physical exam I was diagnosed
with a very serious ailment. To make things
worst my doctor told me that I needed surgery
within fifteen days. Then it dawned on me,
that without a job I had no health insurance.
I felt helpless, but not totally helpless. I
knew there was a higher power.

I opened my Bible, and these words of Jesus
got my attention, "Come to me, all you who

labor and are heavily burdened and I will give you rest." Rest? That's what I need. Rest from these haunting worries and anxieties, and from "what if" scenarios. As I bowed down my head in prayer, I knew the good Lord would listen to someone who is heavily burdened; someone who is almost crushed. I only needed to cry out with steadfast faith. Then tears flowed freely.

When I finally surrendered everything to the Son of God, an amazing thing happened! There was a written notice from my employer that read, "Your health insurance coverage is extended for sixty days without cost to you." Sixty days! Yes! That's all I need.

Subsequently, I had my surgery done right away, and soon I was recovering within the sixty-day time frame. Everything went well, and when I recovered, I started looking for work. Amazing! Within thirty days, I found a new job at Kennedy Space Center.

Finally, I found some kind of rest—God's "wings of rest." I was myself again, and I was happy. At the same time, as I usually prayed daily, the words of Psalm 91 hit me:

"He will surely keep you safe from all hidden dangers, and from all deadly diseases. He will cover you with his wings, you will be safe under his care; his faithfulness will protect and defend you." Obviously hidden within this prayer is inner peace and joy.

Change

Gerry was a middle-aged drug addict who was in and out of rehab. He really wanted to change his ways and get well, but he could not do it without help.

One day, a humble and loving Christian Pastor visited him at the rehab center. Gerry was open to anything that could free him from his addiction. He listened to what the Pastor had to say, and soon they became friends. At one point the Pastor suggested that they pray together, which they did. Subsequently, Gerry admitted that for the first time he felt the presence of God and His astonishing love. That night before going to bed, he opened his heart to God and prayed, "Jesus, please help me." He kept repeating this prayer until he fell asleep. When he woke up the next morning, he realized that he had no longer any craving for drugs. He was totally healed.

When the Pastor returned a couple of days later, Gerry with great elation related his miraculous recovery. Then the Pastor asked him:

"That was a big change. Do you expect any more changes in your life?" Thoughtfully the former addict replied, "Yes, I hope to have many good changes in my life. I believe that there is no limit to change. As long as I have this love for Jesus in my heart, I can change for the better. Like not looking back or blaming anyone. Like making amends with those I have hurt. Like being more kind and understanding. Like desiring to come closer to Jesus."

Obviously love can impact and change a person's perspective in life. It can also impact one's thinking and actions. Why? Because no man remains quite the same when he encounters pure love. And to encounter pure love is to encounter radical change which bears good fruit. But is there a limit to this process? No! Why? Because there is no limit to love. And since God is love, his unlimited and boundless nature remains. There is no limit to positive change. There is no limit to grace. There is no limit to spiritual happiness. So, what are you waiting for? Make yourself happy, and make Jesus happy too. Change for the better.

Divine Providence

St. Augustine once said, "For if the providence of God does not preside over human affairs, there is no point in busying oneself with religion."

Some people do not buy into divine providence. They think that God has no say in the way we live our lives. They think that we are left alone to our own devises. However, God does surprisingly enter into our lives. He does this with purpose, either to straighten our lives, to call us to work in the vineyard, or to surprise us with a favor.

In the gospel story, where Jesus walks into the lives of Peter, James and John while they were busy getting ready to go fishing, the Lord simply calls them to follow Him. Jesus said to them, "Come after me and I will make you fishers of men."

They did not fully understand what He meant, but aided by grace, they dropped everything they were doing, and said, "Yes, we will follow

you." Why? Because they saw something excep-
tional and attractive in Jesus. It was His
sincere and bubbling love for them. And once
they said "Yes," Jesus began to write the story
of their lives in a new and exciting way. From
the story of an ordinary fishermen, they would
be transformed into fearless fishers of men, or
ambassadors for Christ. They would become bold
evangelizers motivated by His love.

The main point is: Divine Providence does
preside over human affairs. Divine Providence
does preside over your life. Why? Because
you are precious in His eyes, and He loves
you. He wants an exciting life for you with a
happy ending. That's why He wants to write the
story of your life—if you let Him. However,
if you are too busy writing your own story of
acquiring power, prestige, and possessions,
then the ending would be your own creation.
So why not surrender your life to Jesus and
be happy. Perhaps you can say, "Lord Jesus,
please, from here on, write the story of my
life. Take over my life. In my daily prayers
tell me about your plans. Also, please give
me the grace to say a big "Yes." If you reach
this point, you will be surprised by inner
peace and joy.

Good and Evil

$\mathcal{L}$ife is about darkness and light; about good and evil. During the time of Jesus many jealous religious leaders tried to trap him by saying that Jesus was in cahoots with Satan (Mark 3:22). However, it did not work, because others witnessed the power of Jesus in healing many people, convincing them that his power comes from God.

If Jesus acknowledged the existence of supernatural forces or demons, we would be naïve to deny their reality. Teenagers sometimes encounter demons when they dabble with the occult using Ouija boards or "spirit talking boards." The same is true with those who take excessive alcohol, drugs, or practice sinful habits like pornography and gambling. When they do this, they become prime target of the devil's invasion and possession.

Like the Las Vegas shooter, Stephen Paddock, who killed fifty-nine people had an uncontrolled craving for gambling. This brings about depression and temporary insanity caused by the devil's invasion, and consequently becoming suicidal and violent to other people. But what is the root cause? The root cause is serious or grave sin, which greatly offends God. Unfortunately, the secular world has translated sin into a kind of mental imbalance instead of spiritual blindness.

Spiritual blindness prevents a person to distinguish between good and evil, between violence and love. It is being out of touch with God, and therefore out of touch with God's holy will. Remember God's holy will is always good for us. It helps us to be the best person we can be. It helps us to build the family of God. That's why Jesus said, "Here are my mother and my brothers. For whoever does the will of God is my brother, and sister, and mother" (Mark 3:34).

Clearly, people who does God's will, belongs to the family of God. Therefore, it is lamentable to be outside of God's holy will. That's why Bishop Fulton Sheen once prayed, "I know dear Lord how crosses are made. Your holy will is the vertical bar, and my will is the horizontal bar. When I place my will against your will, I make a cross. *Grant that I may make you no more crosses.*"

Looking back, think how many crosses we made for Christ because of our shortcomings and grave sins. Thank God we have confession. Because of this beautiful sacrament our spiritual eyes are opened, and we are drawn closer to the Son of God. As a result, our love for God blossoms and intensifies. That's why G. K. Chesterton said, "Love is not blind. Love is bound. The more it is bound, the less it is blind." Perhaps a true story can amplify this tenet.

Nelson Hutchinson, a young lad, lived in a small house with his parents on the Homosassa River, a few miles from the Gulf of Mexico. In 1940, his dad struggled to support the family as a commercial fisherman with a small boat. His mother was a devout Christian who loved to read the Bible and go to church. But she did not own a Bible, because she could not afford one. She set aside a few coins whenever she could, but unfortunately, financial emergencies would come up, and she had to use the few coins she had saved.

One day his dad came home from work with an empty boat; he had caught nothing. He looked defeated. His mother got into the boat, arranged the nets, started the motor, and headed towards the gulf. Along the way she prayed, "Father, I want a Bible for my home, but I don't have the money. Let me catch enough fish today so I can buy one. Please help me."

Arriving at the gulf, she lowered the net and moved the boat in a circle. To her amazement big mullets or fish started jumping into the net. As fast as she could empty the catch into the boat, and lowered it again, the same thing happened—big mullets jumped into the net. In an hour, the boat was filled with fish, almost to the point of sinking. To make a long story short, she went home and called her son to help her take the fish to a wholesaler. That day, she earned much more than the cost of the beautiful Bible that she bought that day. She was happy as a lark, and her gratitude and love for God was without bound. Why? Because love is not blind, it can see and taste the goodness of the Lord. It is bound by her deep faith and trust in God's compassion and mercy.

With this convincing experience, her heart was set on fire by the Holy Spirit. That's why Jesus said, "I have come to light a fire on the earth, I wish the blaze were ignited." (Luke 12:49) Obviously, Jesus is saying, "Away with doubt. Away with shallow and lukewarm love. Away with mediocre love. Live intensely for me each day.

That's why Fr. McNamara keeps our feet close to the fire by saying, "The difference between us and the saints, is that the saints throw themselves into the fire of God's love and emerge burnt, but magnificently transfigured, while the rest of us spend our lives walking around the fire, close enough to be warm, but never so close as to risk being touched by the flames!"

So, what are you waiting for? Throw yourself into the fire of God's burning love for you. As I said earlier: Away with doubt. Away with shallow and lukewarm love. Away with mediocre love. Live intensely for God each and every day. When you do this, you will be happy and find inner peace.

The Resolute Sacred Heart

*G*od's love for us is resolute and unstoppable. It will not rest until He has exhausted all means of drawing us to His Sacred Heart.

One time the Lord used a simple nun, St. Margaret Mary of the Visitation sisters in France, to unfold his divine plan. One night in 1673, as the humble nun was praying before the Blessed Sacrament in the chapel, out of thin air, the Lord appeared to her and said:

"My divine heart is so passionately in love with my people that it can no longer contain within itself the flames of its ardent charity. It must be poured out to them by your means, and manifest itself to them to enrich them with the precious treasures, which contain all the graces of which they have need to be saved from perdition. I have chosen you as an abyss of unworthiness to accomplish so great a design, so that all may be done by me."

St. Margaret at the time, was not certain when and how the good Lord would accomplish this plan. No sooner had she finished her introspections than Jesus asked her a favor. She described it this way:

"He demanded my heart, and I supplicated him to take it. He did so, and taking it from my chest He placed it into his own adorable and flaming heart. Then he allowed me to see my heart as a little atom, being consumed in that fiery furnace of love. Then drawing it out like a burning flame in the form of a heart, he placed it back into my chest saying: 'Behold my beloved, a precious proof of my love. I enclose in your heart, a little spark of the most ardent flame of my love to serve you as a heart, and to consume you until your last moment. Until now you have taken only the name of my servant; henceforth you shall be called the beloved disciple of my Sacred Heart.'"

Wow, what a precious gift! A heart inflamed with the love of God. How I wish we could all be set on fire with the love of the Sacred

Heart. Subsequently, St. Margaret Mary became the instrument of the Sacred Heart to propagate the devotion throughout Europe and the rest of the world.

Note that most of the priest, nuns, lay leaders, and parishioners I know have some kind of a devotion to the Sacred Heart. I must confess that my ministry started after I have completed my nine consecutive first Friday devotion to the Sacred Heart. If you have not done this, I highly urge you to do it. Why? Because I assure you that there is a hidden secret in store for you, if and when you complete this devotion. The many surprising "miracles" I have experienced in practicing this devotion still mystify me. The result is a deep and faithful love for the Son of God. Doing this will flood your heart and soul with tremendous joy. You will be happy!

The Author of My Life

From nothing God created me into being. So was you. Why? Some say to be a doctor, a teacher, an engineer, a priest or a nun. But perhaps that's just a profession or a vocation of your choice.

Lately, while remembering the roller coaster ride of my life, I've come to the conclusion that in the end, God is writing the story of my life.

I didn't see or pick up on the author then, because I was so intense in living life. I thought I was writing my own charming story. But when I look back now on my days in Manila, later in San Francisco, and now in Winter Park, Florida, I can see the invisible pen of God chronicling my life story. And He does yours, too, if you obey Him and let His divine plan or Holy Will be accomplished in your life. Yes, He will plan it and take care of the details if you let Him.

However, we must learn decentralization, meaning to take our selfish egos and our paranoid desire to control, out of our ego-system, and let Jesus be the focus and center of our attention. This is really centering and giving our lives to God.

One time Mother Teresa of Calcutta was interviewed by a reporter who asked her how she copes with running her vast organization around the world. She smiled and said, "I pray."

"So what do you do when you run out of resources?"

"I go to Jesus," Mother Teresa replied.

"What do you do if your nuns get sick?"

"I go to Jesus."

"What do you do if the Bishop does not agree with your ideas?"

"I go to Jesus."

Obviously, Mother Teresa is so spiritually centralized that she takes everything to Jesus. Jesus is the center of her vision and the center of her conscience. He is her hero, her champion, her Savior, her Beloved. That's why Mother Teresa does not micromanage her life; she lets Jesus do that. In this way, she can be free to love the poorest of the poor or any person in front of her. She knows that life is full of endless interruptions beyond her control, and it is best to let Jesus handle the details.

This too, is another secret of a happy life: Let Jesus micromanage your life.

Let Jesus write the story of your life. Surrender your free will and your tenacious control habits to someone who can assure you of a happy ending. After all, in the end, the bottom line is: Give Jesus your heart, your life, and your free will. When you do this, you are letting God write the story of your life. Be assured, it will have a happy ending.

A Truly Happy Heart

When Gab, my granddaughter, was tiny and little, her greatest joy was to be cradled in her mother's arms. It was like she was in heaven when she was loved by her mom and dad. When she was placed in her crib, she would sob and cry. There was nothing compared to being cradled in love.

Then later in life, when she discovered toys, TV, and trinkets, her source of joy and happiness varied like the seasons of the year. Yes, she still wanted to be hugged and kissed by her parents, but not for a long time; she had other things to do.

One day I called her on the phone, she was now ten years old. We had this conversation:

"Are you happy?"

"No!"

"Why?"

"Because I am going to another school, and I don't like that school. Besides my friends are not going there."

"Is it a Catholic school?"

"Yes."

Silence followed. Then I somehow saw her problem. I told her:

"Gab, your school is not your happiness. God is your happiness. Your love for God and His love for you is your happiness. Remember when you were little, your joy was being loved by your mom and dad. It is the same; as long as you love God and God loves you, you should be happy. Jesus should be your happiness! Knowing that Jesus loves you is a tremendous source of joy."

Somewhat enlightened she simply said, "OK." I took a sigh of relief and lifted my eyes to the heaven's giving praise to God.

Today we see people with misplaced source of happiness. Some stake their happiness in material success, power, prestige, and possessions. If you take even a sliver of these things away from them, they become unhappy and miserable. In the same way, if the Dow goes down, they are unhappy; but if it goes up, they are jubilant. As we say, they are probably spiritually blind.

It is not a secret, if we love God we are happy. If we serve Him, we are happier. If we come closer to Him each day, we are unstoppable.

The Transparent Rose

$\mathcal{S}$he is the ambassador of Divine Mercy! Sister Faustina Kowalska was born in Lodz County, Poland, in 1905. At the age of 15 she humbly asked her parents to allow her to enter the convent. Thus began the breathtaking journey of a transparent soul, indeed a transparent rose for the garden of heaven. Mystical and interior consolations were showered upon her by the Son of God, and as always she would respond with sheer honesty, with no hidden agenda—spontaneously speaking from her heart.

Thus, I would say, the heavens salute her as the "Transparent Rose."

In her Diary, she records a poignant and touching moment of humble conversation with the Son of God.

Jesus, "My daughter, if you wish, I will this instant create a new world, more beautiful than this one, and you will live there for the rest of your life."

Sr. Faustina, "I don't want any worlds. I want you Jesus. I want to love you. I want to love you with the same love that you have for me. *I beg you for only one thing, to make my heart capable of loving you.* I am very much surprise of your offer, my Jesus. What are those worlds to me? Even if you gave me a thousand of them, what are they to me? You know very well, Jesus, that my heart is dying of longing for you. *Everything that is not you is nothing to me.*"

Pure. Unadulterated. Simple. Totally transparent response of pure love from the saint. I know I could say those words too. But then it is not my words, and the offer of love was not to me.

But pure love has endless variety of expression. At times, it is a flash of unrestrained certainty and joy because Jesus loves us back. At times, it is simply pure unfathomable beauty of total dependence in God. Nonetheless, the hidden fragrance is in its transparency.

Transparent love is the joy and happiness we can relish now, if we but give our hearts to the Son of God.

Obedient to Love

*F*r. John Shea once quipped, "Argue with everything but always be obedient to love." Why is this statement so compelling? In most cases, it is compelling to people who are truly in love. In the same way, it is also compelling to dedicated and loving parents caring for their little ones. Obviously, arguing is not the issue, it is the depth of one's love and willingness to sacrifice that is the issue. It is the degree of total giving of oneself to the beloved.

During the French revolution government soldiers were rounding up people in a small village who were part of the resistance—they were referred to as rebels. The soldiers found a mother with her two children hiding under a big hedge. Immediately the soldiers noticed that they were starving—they have not eaten for days. Since the revolution was over, the soldiers gave the mother a few pieces of bread. Without hesitation, the mother divided the meager ration between her two children. She herself did not partake of the bread. Obviously, she was obedient to love, to the unselfish love of a mother for her children. The soldiers noticed that there was a grin in her face. She has found true happiness.

On another level, we probably should note that love is an impulse. Mystics realize that this impulse to love comes from God. It is a gift to witness the reality of God's love in the world. And what's wonderful, is that this impulse of pure love is a great source of happiness.

The next time you feel like helping someone who feels abandoned or helpless, or is in great need, simply be obedient to love. And if you do it and extend a helping hand, you will feel a surge of inner joy. Unknowingly, you have tapped into the source of true happiness.

Engaging Presence

A mystic once said that *love is a never-ending presence*. If we think about this in a human level, this is unachievable. But in the level of the heart, in the level of consciousness, this is possible . . . a never-ending presence.

Even if you are too busy with mundane things, but your heart is awake and your spiritual eyes are open, then presence to the One you love is pure joy and life. And who is this One you love? It is the Son of God.

That's why the famous monk Brother Lawrence of France noted, "The practice of the presence of God is the shortest and easiest way to attain the Christian perfection. It is the form and life of virtue."

On a practical level, what does he mean by this? Brother Lawrence explained, "For me the *time of activity does not differ from the time of prayer,* and in the noise and clatter of my kitchen, while several people are together calling for as many different things, I possess God in as great a tranquility as when upon my knees at the Blessed Sacrament." Surely it appears that in the domain of relationship, *"presence," means possession of the One we love in our hearts."*

Note that Brother Lawrence does not live his life in compartments. It is a life of uninterrupted and engaging awareness of the presence of the beloved Son of God. It is the intensity of his love that makes the difference. That's why he emphatically pointed out that *the presence of God can be reached more readily by the heart* rather than the intellect or understanding. In his words, "In the way of God, thoughts count for little, love is everything." That's why the mystic and saint Teresa of Avila said, *"The important thing is not to think much, but to love much, and so to do whatever best awakens us to love."*

Basically, our goal is to awaken ourselves to the love of the Crucified One. The One who's love is so intense, so great, and so redeeming, that he took upon himself our iniquities and transgressions. For indeed Jesus redeemed us for himself. He loved us unto death. He reconciled us for heaven.

And for us, what is our response? Consider this. *There is no remedy to love but to love*

even more. When we follow this impulse of love
and perpetual presence, then happiness is just
arounds the corner.

Reaching for Holiness

*H*oliness is a big word. Like a prism, there are many ways of expressing itself. However, our Catechism tells us, "It is doing the will of the Father in everything for His glory—and in service of his neighbor. In some ways, this is accomplished through spiritual progress through ever more intimate union with Christ."

In addition, our Catechism tells us, "The way of perfection passes by way of the cross. There is no holiness without renunciation and spiritual battle." And St. Gregory of Nyssa adds, "He who climbs never stops going from beginning to beginning, through beginnings that have no end. He never stops desiring what he already knows."

Yes, as believers, we desire holiness. For Mother Teresa of Calcutta this means doing everything for the love of God. This also means for her, striving toward ever greater humility.

To manifest holiness in a more reflective way she wrote this prayer:

> Breath in me, O Holy Spirit, that my thoughts may all be holy.
> Act in me, O Holy Spirit, that my work, too, may be holy.
> Draw my heart, O Holy Spirit, that I love but what is holy.
> Guard me then, O Holy Spirit, that I always may be holy. Amen.

Now, this manifestation of holiness in thoughts, work, and genuine love, inevitably blossoms into inexplicable joy.

One time, a beggar approached Mother Teresa and said, "Mother Teresa, everybody gives you things for the poor. I also want to give something. But today, I am only able to get ten pence. I want to give that to you."

The holy nun thought, "If I take it, he might have to go to bed without eating. If I don't take it, I will hurt him." She took it. Mother Teresa was amazed at the tremendous joy expressed in the beggar's face. She never forgot the incident. She later said, "This is the joy of loving."

Is it possible then, that holiness is simply the joy of loving Jesus? Like a prism, there are myriads of ways, big and small, of loving the Son of God. Why do we miss so many opportunities? What robs us of this joy? Ponder on this.

Believing without Seeing

When I was in college, as most men do, I dreamed of getting married and raising a family. I dreamed of finding the right partner in life and living a fulfilling life. It was all in my head, but deep within me I believed that I would someday meet this special person. Without seeing, I believed that someday, I would meet the love of my life. And it happened, I did meet the right person, got married, and raised a family.

An atheist is different. They usually do not believe in things they do not see. They must be able to use all their senses to confirm the existence of a person, place, or thing. I once read a story and it went like this:

An atheist had a friendly conversation with a Christian believer. He said, "Prove to me the existence of God and I will become a Christian."

The believer responded, "But you are a minority in this world, there's not too many of you. Prove to me that there is no God, and I will be an atheist."

The atheist was silent for a moment and then said, "I can't."

"Amazing," the believer exclaimed. "You believe in something that you cannot prove! By your own criteria, then you will never know the truth. But for me, since I believe, in faith, that there is a God, then I will forever rejoice in this knowledge. And my benevolent and loving God will take me to His Kingdom where I can be happy forever. Unlike you, I have found the truth."

For most of us, not only did we find the truth, but we have also found Jesus, who is the way, the truth, and the life. Like my believing that I will find a good wife, I also believe that I will meet the Lord and see Him face to face at some point in time.

As a mystic once said, "The virtues of faith, hope, and love are supernatural gifts that lead the soul to God." And as Jesus said, "Blessed are those who have not seen and yet believe." That's why we understand, that it is because of faith, that we exchange the present for the future. So smile and be happy because you know the truth—Jesus is Lord. And the truth will set you free.

Prayer Moves the
Hand of God

Many times, we try everything we can to make things happen. Sometimes we want it spontaneously, other times we give it some time. On our own, it is simply a trial and error basis, or a hit and miss process. Oftentimes, we have no basic framework to work with, we simply hope for the best to happen.

Consider this. To get things done we simply need to know that "Prayer moves the hand that moves the world." Whether it is an emergency or a long lingering problem, the mantra is; "Prayer moves the hand that moves the world."

St. Columbanus, a revered Irish monk, was traveling alone in the forest. He was on his way to visit one his monasteries.

Suddenly, a pack of twelve wolves surrounded him, ready to tear him to pieces. Calmly, and with confidence, he looked up to the heavens and prayed, "Incline into my aid, O God. O

Lord, make haste to help me." As he finished his prayer, the pack of wolves fled.

Miraculous! Instant, spontaneous prayer answered without delay. Indeed, "Prayer moves the hands that moves the world." Whether facing a Goliath or a pack of wolves, to know this simple principle by heart can make us rejoice in God's goodness and mercy. Likewise, we can be happy as we place our trust in Him.

The Faith of a Child

*S*r. Kalyani became my friend. She used to work for Mother Teresa in the adoption center of the Sisters of Charity in India. Now she is retired confined to a wheelchair challenged by paralyzed legs. Her relatives brought her to Florida. One day she told me this story.

When she was a postulant in Calcutta, she slept with five other nuns in a room. In the middle of the room was a big wall clock to help them to be on time for mass, adoration, and other activities. But one day it broke down, and they felt somewhat helpless. Who would keep time? They were not allowed to wear wrist watches. Fortunately, there was a small statue of St. Joseph in their room, and they decided to invoke his help; after all they had a devotion to the saint.

First they drew a picture of a wall clock on a piece of paper and placed it under the statue with the words, "Please, we need this."

That night, they began their nine-day novena prayers to St. Joseph.

On the second day of their novena, there was a middle-aged woman who knocked on their door, saying, "While I was praying, I was given the impression to give you this old clock of mine since I just bought a new one." Sr. Kalyani told me that the donated clock lasted for several years. Also, she added that St. Joseph is a humble intercessor and a quiet provider for the nuns.

Wow! What childlike trust and confidence the nuns had in St. Joseph's assistance. After all, as I often say, "Love is a miracle because it is always willing to do the impossible."

Pure Love is Life

There's a story told about William Frey from Colorado, who volunteered to read for a student named John who was blind. One day he asked John, "How did you lose your sight?"

He answered, "A chemical explosion, at the age of thirteen."

William continued, "How did that make you feel?"

John sighed and said, "Life was over for me. I felt helpless. I hated God. For the first six months, I did nothing to improve my lot in life. I would eat all my meals alone in my room. One day my father entered my room and said, 'John, winter's coming. The storm windows need to be up, and that's your job. I want those hung by the time I get back.'"

"Then my dad walked out of the room and closed the door. I got angry. I thought, 'Who does he think I am? I'm blind.'"

"But I was so angry, I decided to do it. I felt my way to the garage, found the windows, located the necessary tools, found the ladder, all the while muttering under my breath, 'I'll show him. I'll fall, and then he'll have a blind and paralyzed son!'"

"So I got the windows up," John continued. "But I found out later that never at any moment was my father more than four feet away from my side. He was always there. And that's when I discovered I could do something better with my life than mope in my room all day. So now here I am in college."

"He was always there," John concluded about his earthly father. So it is with God, our heavenly Father. We may not see Him, but He is always there for us. Thanks to Jesus who made sure we know this by heart, that we have a loving Father in heaven.

In Matthew 11:27, Jesus tells His disciples, "My Father has given me all things. No one knows the Son except the Father, and no one knows the Father except the Son, and to those to whom the Son chooses to reveal him."

Pay attention to what Jesus is challenging us. He alone, by choice, can reveal the Father to us, and He is giving us this opportunity to know the Father; but we must ask Jesus.

We understand that to know Jesus in a personal way makes us happy; would we not be even happier if we also know the Father better? If we dare, let us ask the Son of God, in some humble way, to reveal the Father to us. I believe that Jesus wants us to come closer to the Father too. Why? Because it will make us happy. As we pray, "Abba, Dad, Father, I love you," there will be a new ring of joy to our prayer. Jesus' revelations of the Father will make this happen. Why? Because *pure love of God is life, and pure love is joy.*

The Living Bread

*T*his is a true story. In August 18, 1996 in Buenos Aires, Fr. Pezet was told by his sacristan about a discarded consecrated host (dispensed at Holy Communion) left in a candleholder. Following protocol, he placed the host in a small water container to allow it to dissolve and then placed it inside the tabernacle.

A week later he checked the host, but it did not dissolve. Instead it turned into a bloody fragment of flesh. He then informed Cardinal Jorge Bergoglio, now Pope Francis, who told him to have a professional photographer take picture of the fragment. For several years, the host or bloody fragment remained in the tabernacle under strict secrecy. Subsequently, Cardinal Bergoglio decided to have the fragment scientifically analyzed.

In October 5, 1999, Dr. Castanon, under the direction of the Cardinal, took a sample of the bloody fragment to New York for scientific analysis. He did not tell Dr. Zugiba, the analyst, who was also a cardiologist, where the fragment came from.

After extensive testing, Dr. Zugiba has determined that the bloody host was "a fragment of the heart muscle found in the wall of the left ventricle close to the valves." He also disclosed that "the heart muscle is in an inflammatory condition and contains a large number of white blood cells. This indicates that the heart was alive at the time the fragment was taken, since the white blood cells die outside a living organism. The white blood cells require a living organism to sustain them. Therefore, the presence of white blood cells indicates that the heart was alive when the sample fragment was taken."

Dr. Zugiba continued by saying, "What is noteworthy is that the heart had been under severe stress, as if the person had been severely beaten about the chest."

Later Dr. Castanon, the one who brought in the sample fragment, informed Dr. Zugiba that the analyzed sample fragment came from a consecrated host which is a white unleavened bread.

Dr. Zugiba was in disbelief. "How and why a consecrated host would change its character and become a living human flesh and blood will remain an inexplicable mystery to science."

Yes, a mystery to science but not to believers. This Eucharistic miracle simply attest to our belief of the real presence of Jesus in the Eucharist. Our eyes of faith can see Jesus in the Eucharist even without the miracle. We know that in the Eucharistic Jesus wants to live in us, and he does. I often remind believers, "Jesus, the One you love, lives in you." If this is true, then we should be the happiest person on earth.

I Touched Jesus

Mother Teresa, sometimes referred to as "the angel of the slums" by the people of Calcutta, India, was truly a symbol of God's mercy. Dying old people abandoned in the streets of Calcutta was a common sight. No one paid attention to them since they were relegated as human trash. But not for Mother Teresa and her nuns who would pick them up and cared for them in a place called Kalighat, or home for the dying. As God prospered her humble work, many young women from other countries joined her congregation known as the Missionaries of Charity.

One day a new member of the congregation, or a novice, from another country, was assigned to work at the Kalighat. Before she left, Mother Teresa told her, "You saw Father during Holy Mass and with what love and care he touched Jesus in the Host. Do the same when you go to the Home for the Dying because it is the same Jesus you will find there in the broken bodies of our poor."

At the end of the day, the novice came back to the Mother House with a big smile on her face and said to Mother Teresa, "Mother, I have been touching the body of Christ for three hours!"

Mother Teresa inquired, "How?"

The excited novice replied, "When we arrived there, they brought a man who had fallen into a drain and was there for some time. He was covered with wounds and dirt and maggots, and I cleaned him, and I knew I was touching the body of Christ." Mother Teresa smiled and commended her for her work.

A religious peak experience for the novice? A personal encounter with the Son of God for her? To those who know and had a similar exposure, it speaks volumes. But the spiritual eyes must be opened for this to happen. The heart must be accepting and the truth embedded in it. To touch Jesus among the poor and the needy is to be filled with happiness and joy. And Jesus is available to all who care to touch Him among the poorest of the poor.

True Love Never Ends

Kim Carpenter, a baseball coach, fell in love with Krickett, a lovely gymnast. Theirs was an enchanted affair that ended in an elegant wedding. Life was good.

However, a terrible car accident would change their lives forever. Krickett, the once lovely bride, ended up in the hospital, and later went into a coma. After four months, she woke up from a coma, only to discover that she had lost her memory of the past. She did not recognize her husband, nor feel any affection for him. He was like a complete stranger to her. Their marriage was on hold.

Fortunately, their parents reminded them of their marriage vows: to be faithful to each other in sickness or in health, and in good times and in bad. Being committed Christians, they decided to work things out.

To make things feel right, Kim began the long process of courting and wooing Krickett all over again. They started dating and being together like best friends. In the end, and with patience, Kim won Krickett's heart. Life was good again.

Three years after the accident, Krickett married Kim a second time to the delight of her parents and friends. Today they have two children, Danny and LeeAnn. In the end, everything worked out, because *true love stories never have ending.*

In a similar way, God's covenant with his people, you and I, are irrevocable. His promise of fidelity is timeless. To put it in the simplest form, God is saying to us, "I will love you to no end. I will never turn my back on you." Knowing this loving promise is to experience great joy. The Lord will woo us back again, no matter what it takes. This knowledge is happiness beyond measure. And our challenge each day is simply to be faithful to Jesus to the end.

Interior Happiness

*H*e was kind of short—five feet six inches tall—but Napoleon Bonaparte managed to become the Emperor of France in 1804. Today, when someone is embarrassed for being short, they use the excuse that they have a "Napoleon complex." Altogether though, Napoleon was known for his military genius in the battlefield and his many victories brought him fame throughout Europe.

One day, his generals were discussing the many battles they have won and how Napoleon's strategy lead them to triumph. One general asked the Emperor which was the happiest day of his life, thinking he would mention his victory in Lodi, or in Lombardy, or in Austerlitz, which made him the master of Europe.

Napoleon carefully pondered the question then replied, "Ah, the happiest day of my life? That was the day of my first holy communion. I was near God then."

Unexpected. Beyond the radar. Perhaps even childish. The generals must have been stupefied by the response. But the Emperor spoke the truth. One of his peak religious experience was receiving the Son of God in Holy Communion.

Wow! That makes me proud and jubilant for being a Catholic. I have access to this unbelievable and unforgettable happiness in partaking of the Eucharist. Simply put, Eucharist equals interior happiness.

The more we receive Jesus in Holy Communion the happier we become. That's why St. Faustina Kowalska said, "One thing alone sustains me, and that is Holy Communion; Jesus concealed in the host is everything to me. From the tabernacle, I draw strength, power, courage, and light. Here, I seek consolation in time of anguish. I would not know how to give glory to God if I did not have the Eucharist in my heart."

Unbridled by Sin

St. John Chrysostom was known as the man with the "Golden Mouth," because of his eloquent and masterful preaching. Consecrated as Archbishop of Constantinople (Istanbul, Turkey) in 397 AD, he reformed his priests by instructing them to spend time with the poor and the homeless. With his natural zeal and eloquence, he successfully converted many sinners, including heretics.

Unfortunately, Emperor Arcadius, the ruler at the time, was told a string of lies about Chrysostom that resulted in his persecution and exile. The Emperor consulted with his advisors for the best method to punish Chrysostom.

"Confiscate his property!" said one.

"Whom will that harm?" the Emperor asked. "Not Chrysostom, but only the poor to whom he gives all he has."

"Cast him to prison," said a second advisor.

"What would be the use, he would only glory in his chains," the Emperor retorted.

"Well then, kill him," said another.

"How would that help? It would only open the gates of heaven to him," the Emperor exclaimed.

Finally, one wiser than the rest proposed, "There is only one thing in the world that Chrysostom fears. He is afraid to sin. We must make him sin."

Well, you know the rest of the story. They could not make Chrysostom commit sin, so they simply exiled him to a far and remote place. Unfortunately, on his way to this distant place of exile, since he was already old, he fell ill and went home to God.

Extraordinary! The saint dreaded sin more than death itself. Today, the word "sin" is not even mentioned in newspapers, magazines, or the media. And yet it is real as tea and coffee. It is so real that the consequence of sin is felt almost instantly. Yes, people can hide it, push it away, or ignore it. Nonetheless, it catches up with the sinner, unless the mercy of the Son of God is invoked. And when repentance, followed by God's mercy is received, then peace and happiness is restored.

Upend the World

*B*oris was a young idealistic Russian con-
scientious objector. After reading the
New Testament and absorbing its true meaning,
he began to question the ideals of the Bolshevik
maxims. Soon his disturbing messages to the
Russian elite got him into trouble.

He was brought before the magistrate to
explain his thinking and behavior. With firmness and conviction, he tried to convince the
judge of the beauty of loving one's enemies,
or overcoming evil with good, and bringing
about peace and not war.

The judge understood Boris' argument and
said, "Yes, I get your point, but you must be
realistic. These ideals you are talking about
are the laws of the kingdom of God; and it has
not come yet."

After a moment of silence, Boris spoke up
with conviction and fervor. "Sir, I recognize
that it has not yet come for you, nor for
Russia, but the kingdom of God has come for

me! I cannot go on hating and killing as though it had not come."

The judge was taken by surprise at the response. Clearly this statement has upended the judge's premise. The battle for the pre-eminence of the kingdom of God has challenged the reality of the judge's world.

On a deeper level, Origen, an early church father tells us, "According to our Lord and Savior, the kingdom of God does not come in such a way as to be seen. No one will say, 'Look, it is here!' or 'There it is!' because the *kingdom of God is within us.* The Word is very near us; it is on our lips and in our hearts."

Absolutely true: the kingdom of God is within us. *It is the kingdom of the Son of God.* It is the kingdom of goodness, beauty, and truth.

Puppy Love

*J*orge Bergoglio of Argentina, known today as Pope Francis, was a lover of the poor and an ambassador of God's mercy. He was also known for his humility and simplicity. Nonetheless, as a young boy of twelve, his heart was pulled in a different direction by a young girl, his best friend. Amalia Damonte was her name, and the young Jorge had a crush on her.

With good intentions, Jorge sent her a letter with a picture of a house, indicating that this would be their domicile when they get married. Unfortunately, the letter was discovered by Amalia's parents. Considering their young age, the parents were amused, and displeased with Jorge's proposal. Subsequently, a strong disapproval of their friendship followed.

The next day the two friends met. With childlike simplicity, Amalia sadly narrated the episode about her parents disapproval. Jorge was silent, then with measured firmness said, "If you can't marry me, then I'll become a priest."

Was this the hand of God? Was Jorge being groomed for something bigger? At that time, we would not know. But today we can confidently say "Yes." Divine Providence or the hand of God can lead us to a new horizon.

The Flower of the Ghettos

*M*other Teresa, often referred to as the "living saint of Calcutta" who opened the first hospice for the dying was known to be sensitive to the various religious persuasion of those she cared for. Therefore, respecting their personal beliefs, the sisters would read the Quran to the Muslims, give the Hindus water from the Ganges (considered holy), and for Catholics they would invite a priest to administer the last rites. Their goal was to have each one of them experience a "beautiful death"; although they may have lived like animals on the streets, hopefully they would die like angels . . . loved and wanted by the sisters.

One time, Mother Teresa, alongside a visitor, pointed to the rows of patients resting in pallets or stretchers and said to the visitor:

"Our work calls for us to see Jesus in everyone. He has told us that He is the

hungry one. He is the naked one. He is the thirsty one. He is the one without a home. He is the one who is suffering. These are our treasures. They are Jesus. Each one is Jesus in His distressing disguise; Jesus in His distressing disguise."

Mother Teresa has her spiritual eyes wide, wide open. If we can even approach this deep vision of love and charity, we can be happy.

Love is Always a Choice

Princess Alice was the daughter of Queen Victoria of England. She had a four-year-old son whom she loved so much. But one day her son got sick with a deadly and contagious disease known as "black diphtheria." The nurses told her to stay away from her son to avoid contamination. But one morning, as the Princess watched her son in a far corner of the room, she heard her son ask the nurse, "Why doesn't my mother kiss me anymore?" This was more than the Princess could bear, so with tears in her eyes, she ran to her son, picked him up, and showered him with kisses.

This turned out to be the kiss of death. The Princess contracted the disease, and in a matter of weeks, both mother and son were buried side by side. Was this a foolish act? Perhaps. But whoever said that love is logical?

Look at the Crucified One, bleeding to death on the cross. To a pagan or unbeliever, what Jesus did with all the power at his fingertips appears to be nonsensical. But to Jesus, it was the best thing he ever did. Why? Because He loves us deeply and intensely. Also, because He knows that love is a choice; and He chose to love us without limit. That's why a mystic once said that love is never stingy, that it trembles when it thinks it has given so little." This points to the nature of love which is self-denial, sacrifice, or giving up something for a higher purpose.

I remember the time when I asked my grandson what he offered up for Lent. He said, "I offered up complaining. Instead, I try to say something nice about other people."

I told him, "I'm so proud of you."

Then he told me about Sharon, his classmate who offered up talking for forty days. She did this with the cooperation of her teachers at Bishop Moore High School, her parents, and her classmates. To avoid irritating others, she carried a writing tablet to answer important questions. What a good choice of sacrifice for Lent.

After the Lenten season both Sharon and my grandson felt more centered in God and much happier.

Our Greatest Potential

After Jesus rose from the dead, he surprised his gloomy apostles by appearing to them on the seashores of Lake Tiberias and invited them to have breakfast with him. After breakfast, Jesus asked Peter three times; "Do you love me?" To this, Peter responded, "Yes Lord, you know that I love you." Satisfied, Jesus then reminded Peter of his mission by saying, "Feed my lambs, tend my sheep."

So therein lie our greatest potential; to love God intensely and to bring souls to Him without counting the cost. Obviously, our capacity to love is linked with our capacity to serve. Why? Because we cannot love and be selfish. We cannot love and not be of service to others. That's why Jesus said, "The greatest among you is the servant of all." Obviously, this service is linked with our deep love of God. Without an intense love of God, helping others would be difficult.

This reminded me of what Jesus said to the holy nun and mystic Mary of the Trinity. Jesus said to her, "What does all the rest matter? Am I not with you? Then you will listen to me, then you will console me, then you will speak to me, then you will love me." Clearly, Jesus' ultimate desire is for us to fall in love with Him. Why? Because Jesus is lovesick for us. Yes, the Son of God, the One who died for us on the cross is lovesick for us. Because we are too busy doing other things, Jesus wants us to be aware of His loving presence.

Researchers give us the following statistics of how most working people spend their time on average:

Sleeping and grooming, 7.8 hours.
Commuting and working, 8.5 hours.
Housework and leisure, 4.2 hours.
Watching TV and reading, 3.2 hours.
Praying, 15 minutes.

No wonder Jesus is so lovesick for us! We give Him only fifteen minutes each day. But there is really something more profound that is often overlooked. Consider what Jesus later said to the mystic Mary of the Trinity, "Yes, work is a great dignity, but what I desire is not merely your work, but yourself." Wow! There it is again, Jesus wants you! All of you!

On one occasion, I was speaking to a very active parishioner who was involved in a bunch of church ministry. She told me that often she was exhausted when she got home. Then I asked her if she was happy. She replied, "Somewhat."

I reminded her, "You should be bubbling with joy with all that good work that you do for the Lord." She groaned and said, "I wish. But I don't feel as close to God right now. I'm tired." I mentioned the words of Jesus to the mystic Mary of the Trinity, "Work is a great dignity, but what I desire is not merely your work, but yourself." Then I gently asked her, "Have you given your heart to Jesus lately? How often did you say I love you Lord? How much intimate and quality time did you spend with Him?

She was silent. Moments later, she said, "Thank you for your words, "*I have forgotten the object of my love.*" Note what she said, "I have forgotten the object of my love." And that's the crux of the problem.

"You can trip over love, but if you fall in love, you fall forever." That's what Jesus desires, that we fall in love with Him without ceasing. In the final analysis, to love Jesus unceasingly, is our greatest potential.

Practicing this will bring us inner joy and profound happiness. As Jesus said to the holy nun and mystic, Consolata Betrone, "Love me and you will be happy. The more you love me, the happier you will be." Remember this secret of happiness.

Limit Not God's Grace

*B*e not afraid to ask for God's favor. The Son of God knows the nature of human needs and desire. There is no need to exaggerate or underplay our desires. State them as we actually need them.

Once a blind man begged St. Padre Pio (Italian mystic) to restore his sight, even just in one eye to enable him to see his love ones. The humble padre asked, "Only in one eye?" To which the man responded, "That would good enough." Smiling, the padre concluded, "I shall pray for you."

Weeks later the man returned overjoyed, thanking Padre Pio for his cure. "So are you seeing normally again?" the padre inquired. "Yes, just from this one eye," the healed man answered. Padre Pio admonished, "Ah, only from one eye. Let that be a lesson to you. *Never put limitations on God. Always ask for the big grace.*"

Personally, most of the time I ask for what I basically need, I never underplay my wants. However, when praying for others, I usually inflate my requests. To balance things out however, I usually end up saying, "Only if it is your desire Lord."

There's something about an honest prayer. God always sees our intention and the depth of our love. As Jesus said to the mystic and saint Faustina Kowalska, "I will tell you most, when you converse with me in the depths of your heart, you profit more, than if you had read many books. So, speak to me about everything in a simple way. The simpler your prayer is, the more you attract me to yourself."

Prayer can make us happy and oftentimes give us hope and inner peace.

From the Tomb, He Rose

As Christians, we know that Jesus rose from the dead, and we commemorate this holy event on Easter Sunday. Our scripture tells us that more than five hundred people saw the risen Lord (1 Corinthians 15). After Jesus' resurrection, he did not go straight to heaven; instead he stayed a while—for fifty days—and appeared many times to his friends and disciples. Why? To give them hope, inspire them, and motivate them to accomplish their mission.

Still, today, many do not believe in the resurrection. But here's what Charles Colson who was involved with Nixon's Watergate scandal says about the resurrection, and I paraphrase.

"I know the resurrection is a fact, and Watergate proved it to me. How? Because eleven of the apostles, testified they had seen Jesus raised from the dead, then they boldly proclaimed that truth for forty long years, never once denying it. They were beaten, tortured, stoned and put in prison. They would not have endured that if it weren't true. They were willing to die for the truth of the resurrection.

However, Watergate embroiled eleven of the most powerful men in the world, and they couldn't keep a lie for three weeks. Their cover up did not work. Don't tell me that eleven apostles could keep a lie for forty long years! That's impossible."

The reality of the resurrection is the most significant event in human history. It changes the face of death for all believers. Death is no longer a prison, but a doorway into heaven and into God's presence. And when Jesus appeared to the apostles in the Upper Room, he said to them, "Look at my wounds, it is I. Touch me, touch my wounds." Jesus could not bear their loneliness, their waning faith, and their moving into a kind of lukewarm love. He was going to set their hearts on fire again. Why? To prepare them for their purpose in life which is to image Jesus in this world and to spread the Gospel.

One time Mother Teresa was invited to speak to a big crowd in Washington, DC. Her message was simple but profound; that Jesus is the way, the truth, and the life. However, when she told them, "Jesus loves you," the people were deeply touched. Many became teary eyed. It was as if Jesus was speaking through her; they saw Jesus alive in her. Therefore, this is part of our mission: to reflect Jesus alive in us.

Remember, when we are dealing with awkward and difficult situation, silently pray: Lord Jesus come to life in me, and use me as you desire. When we do this, our hearts begin to sing.

Two Ways of Knowing

*B*asically, there are two ways of knowing. First is through the intellect, reason, or the mind. The mind knows through analysis, by breaking things down and putting it back together again. When we do this, we know we are close to reality.

The second knowing is through the heart. The heart signals this via powerful feelings, emotions, and inspiration. However, to be assured, the heart needs to enter into prayer and contemplation. This contemplation is simply the lifting up of our hearts and souls to a loving God. When we do this, we are illuminated.

That's why in making personal decisions there is always the struggle between the mind and the heart, or between the intellect and emotions. Let's try to understand this via a true story.

Emily was born with beauty and wealth in the big city of Manila, Philippines. Well educated and gregarious, she had many handsome and wealthy suitors. Finally, she was matched by her parents with an educated, rich, and good-looking young man. However, the match was not a perfect one, because Emily was not enamored or attracted to the young man. The reason? They had incompatible personalities.

On a beautiful Sunday morning, as Emily went to church, she met an ordinary, humble, and respectful young man. His name was Efren. They developed an instant rapport and liking for each other. The only problem was that Efren was paralyzed from the waist down. Despite this handicap, he was an excellent educator and admired by his peers. Likewise, his courteousness and happy disposition attracted Emily.

Eventually, love took its course. Emily was attracted to Efren's honesty, humility, and piety. She felt close to God when she was with him. Similarly, Efren was attracted to Emily's beauty, charm, and sincerity. He felt accepted and dignified when he was with her.

Soon, Emily's parents knew about this blossoming friendship, and they tried everything in their power to break up the relationship. Threats and bribes were offered to Efren, to no avail. Why? Because Efren was now deeply in love with Emily, and nothing could make him change his mind. As the saying goes, true love never gives up.

What happened? Did true love prevail? Yes. Eventually, Emily and Efren got married in the church where they met. This was shocking to the parents and to a lot of rich and famous people in Manila. Yes, true love never fails.

That's why St. Thomas Aquinas said in his "Summa"; "The intellect listens to the emotions. The mind is made to serve the heart." To this we can easily add; because the heart is programmed to seek the highest good which is pure love. Unfortunately, the mind alone cannot fully reach God. It is the mind, in harmony with the heart, and guided by faith, that can truly reach God. No wonder it is so important to lift our hearts to Jesus in prayer and contemplation. Why? If the heart is lifted up to God, the heart, with its feelings and emotions, will convince the mind to follow. Subsequently, when the mind and the heart are in harmony, the person's free will is activated and many good, positive actions follows.

"Yes, I will follow you Lord, I will do good," we sometimes say in prayer. The mind and the heart has moved the person to express this intention. If there is harmony, there will be inner peace and joy. When this happens,

it is usually a sign that we are doing God's
will. And again our heart will sing.

Know Thyself

St. Teresa of Avila once said, "Without self-knowledge spiritual growth is not possible." This is a gem of a spiritual advice. For those who seek spiritual awakening and positive change this is an eye opener. Nonetheless, self-knowledge can be deceiving.

Remember St. Peter, "the rock"? He thought he knew himself pretty well. In fact, he was bragging to Jesus that he would be willing to die for him anytime and anywhere. Unfortunately, when Jesus was arrested and brought to trial, Peter lied about knowing Jesus when a lowly servant accused him of being a disciple of Jesus. You know the rest of the story, Peter betrayed Jesus three times. Later, acknowledging his weakness, Peter wept bitterly, and sincerely repented of his sin.

How about St. Paul? He wrote to his followers in Rome, "I cannot even understand my own actions. I do not do what I want to do, but I do what I hate. What happens is that I do, not the good I want to do, but the evil, which I do not intend to do." Clearly, the honest St. Paul knows his weaknesses and his dilemma. Good for him, at least he understands his flaws and human nature.

In my younger days, when I was in college, I did not know myself too well, either. I discovered that I did poorly in subjects that I thought I would excel in, and did well in subjects that I thought I would fail. These and many other discoveries simply pointed to my lack of knowledge about myself.

Let's briefly examine ourselves so that we can be the best person we can be in the eyes of God, and ask Him for assistance at the same time.

- Do I know my weaknesses and strengths? Take your time. Perhaps a close friend can help.
- How do I handle criticism, failure, and success? Perhaps a close sibling can assist.
- Am I aware of my obsessions, vanities, and hot buttons? Maybe a love one can help.
- How big is my ego? Am I a habitual braggart? Because of this, do I try to control other people? Perhaps a close acquaintance and co-worker can lend a hand.

- Do I cling to my past hurts? Have I forgiven those who were involved? Perhaps a
  self-examination asking the Holy Spirit
  for enlightenment can be a benefit.
- Finally, how important is God in my life?
  Do I feel that I need Him? Do I have to
  be personally involved with Him? Perhaps
  an honest reflection is appropriate. Take
  more time in discerning this.

Without a doubt, self-examination is an
important process. However, we must also
accept our uniqueness. We are all different in
the way we speak, think, and solve problems.
Indeed, we have all been endowed with our own
peculiar gifts and handicaps. Aware of this,
we must be brave and not fear the challenges
we face in trying to be the best person we can
be for the honor and glory of God.

Here's a metaphor to ponder.

There's this mouse who was afraid of the
cat. Fortunately, a magician took pity on the
mouse and turned it into a cat.

But then the cat saw a dog and was afraid
of it. Again, in kindness, the magician turned
the cat into a dog. However, later that day,
the dog saw a tiger, and the dog was afraid of
the tiger.

Fortunately, once again, the magician took pity and turned the dog into a tiger. Now feeling strong and confident, the tiger roamed the jungle, but then saw the hunter. Instinctively, the tiger was afraid of the hunter, so once again, the tiger sought the magician.

Now the magician, looking sadly at the pleading tiger, threw his hands up in the air, and with a wave of his hands, turned the tiger back into a mouse. Then he said, "There is nothing else I can do for you, my friend, because *you have the heart of a mouse.*"

How about you, do you have the heart of a mouse? Are you constantly afraid of facing the challenges of life? Are you afraid of a relationship with God, or even falling in love with God? Are you not aware that you were made in His image and likeness? Do you not know that you are a son or daughter of God? Try not to live your life as though you have the heart of a mouse. You are a child of God. You can face the future without fear. You can untangle the most complex oddities of life. You can live in total trust in God's love and benevolence. When you believe this, and live in God's Divine Providence, then you are free to live a life of peace, love, joy, and boldness.

Who is Jesus Christ?

*T*hrough the ages, Jesus Christ has been the center of theological debates. Many have mistaken Him for a "false god." Because of their envy, the Pharisees masterminded his death. But Jesus rose from the dead, and the Jewish religious leaders schemed to dishonor him by saying that his body was stolen by his disciples. Even today, only 33 percent of the world's population, or 2.5 billion people, believe Jesus is the Son of God. These believers, you and I, are known to the world as Christians.

Being a Christian, we accept Jesus as true God and true man. This concept is a paradox to the non-believers. However, this truth was affirmed in the Council of Constantinople in the year 553. It basically stated that Jesus had two natures, human and divine, although one person. It is explained in the Catechism (Para 470) as follows:

"Jesus worked with human hands, he thought with a human mind. He acted with a human will, and with a human heart he loved. Born of the Virgin Mary, he has truly been made one of us, like us in all things except sin."

Note that although Jesus was human, he never ceased to be the Son of God. That's why He can forgive sins, walk on water, and calm the sea. He can cleanse the lepers, heal the blind and the lame. He can raise the dead and drive out demons.

However, as a human person, Jesus is like us in all things, except sin. He has never sinned. He was born in a stable in Bethlehem, through Mary, His mother. He was once a baby like us, and wet his diapers, and needed much love and care. He laughed, cried, got hungry, and got tired. He had to learn to walk, work, and help his dad St. Joseph who was a carpenter. He went to church, or the synagogue, and worshipped with his parents. He learned the Torah or the Jewish scripture. He felt the painful accusations, anger, and jealousy of the Pharisees. He encountered the violence and torture of the Roman soldiers. He experienced being abandoned and betrayed by His apostles. He was tempted by the devil like

213

us, but defeated him. He experienced death as all humans do. But being divine, he rose from the dead on his own power. He then established his church on earth and promised to protect it till the end of time. Why? Because he loves you and me to no end. His love is everlasting and unstoppable. Knowing this, it is our duty to keep this divine love burning in our hearts at all times. That's why Mother Teresa of Calcutta said:

"Be careful of all that can block that personal contact with Jesus. The devil may try to use the hurts of life and sometimes your own mistakes to make you feel it is impossible that Jesus really loves you. Not only does he love you, but even more . . . he thirsts and longs for you. He misses you when you don't come close."

I would like to amplify those words of Mother Teresa, "He misses you when you don't come close." Can we come close to Jesus? There are many ways, but here's a simple and unique way.

One of my ministry is visiting nursing homes and homebound people and giving them the Eucharist. Sometimes I conduct communion service in a nursing home where most attendees are octogenarian. As such, they are mostly in wheelchairs, and often half awake. Towards the end of the prayer service, I approach them individually and give them Holy Communion. The challenge is that sometimes they have a hard time opening their mouths, and when they do, as I place the host in their mouths, their saliva is all over my hand. If you are not spiritually awake, you will find this somewhat repulsive, but if you know that this is Jesus disguised as an old man or woman, then the saliva will not bother you. You will simply relish the innocent behavior of these children of God. These wonderful, fresh encounters with the good Lord are moments that bring me closer to him. Fortunately, there are hand sanitizing dispensers around the room, so I have never been sick or infected in these facilities in my years of ministry.

Who then is Jesus Christ? He is the only Son of God, who came into our world to redeem us from sin, and to open the door of heaven for us. He is also, in some mystical way, the poor, the hungry, the marginalized, the elderly, the helpless, and the needy person. When we see this, because our spiritual eyes are opened, then we will be rewarded with inner joy and pure happiness. Again our hearts will begin to sing.

The Pattern of Grace

*M*ost of the greatest spiritual awak-
enings in life have the pattern of
the parable of the prodigal son. It seems to
convey the process of falling away from God,
and then returning to God. The mystical and
overwhelming force behind this is the mercy of
God, or as we often refer to as God's grace.
To experience this gift or unmerited favor
of God is phenomenal. Most often it changes
everything. A quick true story.

Paolo, an Italian businessman, was a fallen
Catholic. On one occasion, he was scheduled to
negotiate a business deal in Foggia, Italy.
His best friend, Eduardo, who cared about his
soul, requested Paolo to make a side trip to
San Giovanni Rotunda to deliver a letter to
Padre Pio. This was really a setup so Paolo
could meet the famous monk and stigmatist;
also to encounter God's grace in the process.

After consenting to the request, Paolo went
to San Giovanni Rotunda monastery to deliver

the letter personally to Padre Pio. At the sacristy, he was asked to wait for the monk. Upon his arrival, Padre Pio asked him, "Now, what do you want?"

Paolo explained about his friend's letter.

"Ah, yes, the letter. But what about you? Don't you want to go to confession? The monk asked.

Paolo, surprised, admitted he had not gone to mass for a long, long time. He tried to avoid the question, but Padre Pio looked at him intensely as if he saw all the serious sins in Paolo's soul.

Padre Pio said, "How long do you intend living in this disgusting kind of life?"

In a flash, Paolo saw the dark state of his soul. Somewhat trembling, he asked the holy priest to hear his confession. After being absolved of his sins, Paolo was so flooded with peace and joy that he decided to stay at San Giovanni Rotunda for the rest of the week. There he spent time in prayer and attending all of Padre Pio's masses.

Note that Eduardo, Paolo's friend, was the instrument used by Jesus to bring Paolo back to the church. The prodigal son came back to eventually give glory to God in worship and in prayer. This reminds us of the words of Jesus to the Italian mystic Consolata Betrone,

"No one can snatch a soul from me. I did not create you for hell, but for heaven. Not as a companion of the devil, but to enjoy me in everlasting love." With this assurance, we can smile and feel the joy and happiness intended for God's children.

Love Never Gives Up

*T*here's a story told about Madame Katharina Tangari; let's just call her Kathy. One day, she and her friend Rosaria visited a famous resort in Carovilli, Italy. In the resort, there was a large villa surrounded by a magnificent garden. This was owned by a wealthy lawyer who was a Freemason or someone who is considered an enemy of the Catholic Church. People who came to visit the villa where not allowed to take any flowers. However, since Rosaria knew the lawyer, they were invited to have coffee with him. Most of the time, they talked about the beautiful flowers in the garden, intentionally avoiding any mention of religion.

However, at one point, the lawyer said to them, "I'm already an old man. I don't have many more years to live. The thought that I must leave this garden some day is quite bitter to me." Then, taking a deep breath, the lawyer continued, "But I made a pact with the devil."

"With the devil?" the two ladies exclaimed.

"Yes. My whole life, I have served the devil well. After my death, he must compensate me by allowing me, every so often, to return to my garden—to my flowers."

"But sir, you don't really want to go to hell?" the ladies protested.

"Yes, yes. The devil is my best friend," the lawyer smiled.

"I can't believe that, sir, I think your best friends are these beautiful flowers of yours." But at that point the conversation ended, and they parted ways.

Later Kathy was thinking, "Poor lawyer he does not have Jesus in his life that's why his life is upside down."

Months later, Kathy, thinking about the Italian mystic Padre Pio, decided to visit him at San Giovanni Rotunda. She went to confession and later talked to him about the lawyer of Carovilli. Padre Pio promised to pray for the lawyer and instructed Kathy to write him immediately to invite him to take advantage of the coming Good Friday and Easter. The holy priest said this would be a good time for the lawyer to be reconciled with Christ.

The next day, Kathy wrote the lawyer, enclosing a picture of the Sacred Heart of Jesus, not knowing that the lawyer was very ill. Then, just after Easter that year, Kathy received a letter from him. Here's a portion of it.

"My good Lady, I remember you and my friend Rosaria when you came to my place. Oh, I would not have imagined then that I would receive your letter, overflowing with goodness, which led me, by its call, to receive Jesus on the occasion of Holy Easter. A similar appeal was often addressed to me by my loved ones, but I must tell you that your letter, which was quite penetrating with Christian spirit, carried great weight in my decision, and on Holy Thursday a friar of St. Francis, brought me Holy Communion and heard my confession." This is truly a happy ending.

This reminds me of what Padre Pio said, "Don't be discourage when you fall, but animate yourself with new confidence and a profound humility. Your becoming discouraged after the fall is the work of the enemy; it means you surrender to Satan and accept that you are beaten. You will not do this, because the grace of God is always vigilant in coming to your aid."

Great advice. Obviously, we can also make the point that pure love, authentic love, never gives up. Because, as Padre Pio said, *God's grace is always vigilant in coming to our aid.*

I often refresh my weak and sometimes broken spirit with this principle when it seems that I am overwhelmed by the challenges of life. That's why I need to pray, go to church, read the Bible, and keep my spiritual eyes open. In this way, I can be assured that love never fails, and it never gives up. This approach makes me a happy camper.

Repent and Believe

$\mathcal{U}$sually during times of protest and violence there is a sense of urgency for calm and repentance. Why? Because the secular world seems to be cluttered with so much animosity and indifference. Just recently in Parkland, Florida, a former student of Marjory Douglas High School shot and killed seventeen people. What seems to be obvious is that without repentance, the spiral of violence will remain unabated. However, to repent, we need some solitude, self-analysis, and focus. That's why we need to disengage from the busyness of this world and take time to examine ourselves and get a sense of what's really going on in our lives. After all, we might be heading the wrong direction and not even know it.

Like what happened to Joe Stack, a software engineer from Austin, Texas who was so miserable and angry at the IRS because he thought he was treated unfairly. He was so angry and miserable that he burned his house down, then boarded his single engine airplane and crashed it into the building where the IRS employees worked. This incident reminded people of the 9/11 terrorist attack. Obviously, Joe failed to slow down and examine his life and spiritual condition. He was always on the fast track. No wonder Plato said, "The unexamined life if not worth living." Also, Joe was not aware of what most psychiatrists say; *all mental illness proceeds from some form of chosen loneliness.* Amazingly, loneliness is a big factor in mental illness. That's why St. Teresa of Avila said, "Without self-knowledge, spiritual growth is not possible." We need to know our shades of loneliness, our miseries, our sins, and bring them all to our merciful God for healing. Hopefully, this will lead us to repentance. That is why Jesus said, "If you do not repent, you will perish." Obviously, there seem to be just one way back to wholeness; repentance and God's mercy and forgiveness. In the end, this will give us inner peace and joy.

Heroic Love

*M*other Teresa of Calcutta does not need any introduction. Since I was young, I always knew her as a saint. What compels me to admire her is her heroic love of Christ. That's why even some of the Hindus in India refer to her as one of their goddess.

Her heroic love was based on an intense and boundless love of God. On her way to the chapel very early in the morning she would silently pray:

"Each sigh, each look, each act of mine, shall be an act of love divine; and everything that I shall do, shall be dear Lord, for love of you."

Then when she would put on her old sandals, she would pray:

"Of my own free will, dear Jesus, I shall follow you wherever you may go in search of souls, at any cost to myself and out of pure love of you."

Now sharing her spiritual goals with the Sisters, she would say:

"Our vocation is not to work with lepers or the dying people; no, *our vocation is to belong to Jesus.* And because we belong to Jesus, like the vine and the branches, we produce fruit in abundance. As long as the branches remain united with the vine, they are capable of bringing forth fruit in abundance.

For Jesus said: 'I am the vine, you are the branches without me you can do nothing.'"

So what makes her heroic? Is it her profound yet simple love of her Beloved Jesus, a love that does not demand anything in return but simply to allow her to continue loving the love of her life; Jesus the Son of God? This joy can be ours too. Obviously, as you watch and observe Mother Teresa, you would notice the exhilarating joy in her face.

Book Knowledge

In the Old Testament, we find that the religious leaders in the time of Jesus were quite knowledgeable of the Torah or Jewish scriptures, yet they were so intent in killing Jesus. It appears that they read the holy book but did not assimilate its spiritual meaning or touched their hearts. Why? Because they were jealous of Jesus' popularity and his healing powers. Obviously, despite their in-depth knowledge of religion, it did not guarantee their acting in a humane and spiritual way.

That's why Pope Benedict XVI once said:

"By itself studying theology doesn't make a person better. It helps to make him better when he doesn't pursue it just as a theory, but tries to get a better understanding of himself, and of man, and of the world as a whole, in what he reads and then tries to appropriate it as a form of life. But in itself, theology is primarily an intellectual occupation, above all when it is pursued with scholarly rigor and seriousness. It can have repercussions on one's attitude as a human being, but it doesn't necessarily make man better, as such."

Wow! This proves the axiom that knowing about Jesus is different from knowing Jesus in a personal way. To encounter Jesus during moments of loneliness and insecurity, and being consoled and strengthened by him becomes an unforgettable experience. It becomes a personal encounter. Also, experiencing Jesus in a life or death situation and coming out on the other side alive and healed, makes him loveable and believable. This kind of knowing Jesus in an intimate way is forever etched in our hearts. It can be the beginning of a lifetime relationship. With this kind of close relationship, we can face life with inner peace and joy.

The Secret

*P*adre Pio is a well-known Italian saint and mystic. He can read people's hearts, bi-locate, is a gifted healer, and famous for being a stigmatist or someone who carries the five wounds of Jesus. Here's a true story that can lift up your heart.

Fr. Placido was a good friend of Padre Pio since they have gone to the same seminary. In 1957 Fr. Placido got seriously ill and was taken to the hospital in San Severo, Italy. One night, out of the blue, he suddenly saw Padre Pio at the foot of his bed. This was not unusual for a saint who can be at two places at one time or bilocation. The visitor told Fr. Placido not to worry about his illness, assuring him of his recovery. The visitor then walked over towards the window, put his hands on the glass window and disappeared in thin air.

The next morning, Fr. Placido feeling rejuvenated, got out of bed and walked towards the window. There he saw the imprint of Padre Pio's hands on the glass. The news of this travelled fast around the hospital and people flocked to his room to see the imprint for themselves. Even those outside the hospital heard about the story and they too flocked to Fr. Placido's room. This created unnecessary traffic in the hospital so the authorities tried to erase and clean off the imprint, but it would not wash away. It was only after a few days later did the imprint disappear.

A new visitor, Fr. D'Apolito, a good friend of Fr. Placido also saw the imprint on the window. Amazed, he told his priest friend that he would ask Padre Pio himself if he left that imprint in the hospital window.

Finally, Fr. D'Apolito made his visit to Padre Pio at the San Giovanni monastery. At the proper time, the good priest asked the saint if he left his finger prints at the hospital window when he made a visit. Padre Pio smiled like a little child and said:

"Yes, I went to the hospital, but don't say anything to anyone." Obviously, the stigmatist was in good humor and wanted to keep things quiet about his "little miracles." Yes, this is the beauty and simplicity of sanctity. It does bring a pleasant surprise; inner happiness and joy.

New Beginning

During the time of Jesus, you would think that the world was falling apart because of the brutality of the Roman soldiers and the ruthlessness of the Jewish religious leaders who were planning to discredit and kill Jesus. In this situation, it appears that evil had the upper hand. Even today there is so much darkness in the world with Christian persecutions and Christian values under assault by non-believers. Nonetheless, in the eyes of Pope Benedict XVI there is always hope. Why? Here's what he said:

"Evil has power via man's freedom, whereby it creates structures for itself. For there are obviously structures of evil. They eventually exert pressure on man; they can even block his freedom, and thereby erect a wall against God's penetration in the world. God didn't conquer evil in Christ, in the sense that evil could no longer temp man's freedom; rather, he offered to take us by the hand, and to lead us. But he doesn't compel us. Apparently, this is the way he wants to rule, that is the divine form of power. And the non-divine form of power, obviously consists in imposing oneself, and getting one's way and coercing. What we know as Christians is that the world, in spite of everything, is in God's hands. Even when man casts off what binds him to God and hastens toward destruction, *God will create a new beginning in the midst of a floundering world."*

Wow! This concept speaks of redemption. Jesus will create a new beginning and a new heart in us in the midst of our floundering. Those who have sincerely repented of their sins at the feet of Jesus knows about the joy and breakthrough of a new beginning. It is a fresh start, as we offer Jesus our fresh committed love.

Obviously, Jesus offers us a second chance, over and over again, until we make it into the Promised Land. Therefore, let us simply thank the good Lord for leading us to his altar of mercy and love, and to strengthen our freedom to be faithful to him to the end.

For we know that true love stories never have endings; and embracing this truth gives us inner peace and joy.

Be Reconciled

*F*or Jesus, reconciliation has something to do with offering gifts at the altar. He mandated that before we offer our gift to God at the altar that we should first be reconciled with our brother or sister whom we may have alienated, and have harbored some resentment. Jesus does not want us to carry a heavy heart when we bring our gifts at the altar. He wants us to be joyful when we approach him.

Why is this? Because even our best personal sacrifices to honor the good Lord would devalue its impact and good intention without first being reconciled with others. As a result, we could be spiritually limping all the way to the altar of God. First, we should be reconciled with God through confession and sincere repentance. Then we should be reconciled with those whom we have alienated or hurt. The goal is to make amends as soon as possible. The obvious reason is that God does not want us to tarnish the gifts we bring to the altar. Also, he wants peace and joy to reign among his people. Unfortunately, there are times when reconciliation does not come easy, especially if we have been deeply hurt.

I remember many years ago when I worked for a boss who was so hard on me. He overloaded me with work, and asked me to come in, an hour early and stay an hour late. I surmised that it was because I became a good friend of his boss and he was jealous. Under such great pressure, I left the company and later found a much better job with a friendlier boss.

However, the hurt was so deep that I had a hard time forgiving my old boss. The confessional was helpful but not fully effective. I prayed for divine assistance. Six months later, I heard from my old friends that my former boss had a heart attack and was now on permanent disability. Suddenly my heart was flooded with compassion for him. I knew how he loved his work, and how he had great expectations for advancement; now it appears that he has reached a dead end.

I had mixed feelings, but mostly compassion and empathy. Immediately I bowed my head and sincerely prayed for him and his family. I also asked the good Lord to forgive me of harboring some ill feelings towards him in the past. Suddenly, I felt freed from this shackle. I realized that resentments are burdens we don't need to carry. Also, I understood that now I could bring my gifts to the altar with pure joy and love.

Remember what St. Francis said; "It is in pardoning that we are pardoned." Likewise note what Mahatma Gandhi advised; "The weak can never forgive. Forgiveness is the attribute of the strong." And to these admonitions we can conclude that happiness are for those who can forgive from the heart and bring their gifts to the altar with perfect joy. When we do this, the invisible Jesus will look upon us with great pride and joy.

Spiritual Blindness

Spiritual blindness is not often a big topic of discussion. Most often people with 20/20 vision would not relish discussing spiritual blindness. Why? Because they are happy with just having a good eyesight. However, we know that spiritual blindness is the worst kind of blindness, which is a kind of deep darkness in the soul and a pathetic ignorance of Jesus Christ.

When I was working at Kennedy Space Center, I use to buy potato chips from a blind man tending the small store. Since he could not see, I would simply hand him the money, which he politely took, and then if I needed some change, he would pull out a basket which was filled with coins and hand it to me. He was kind and courteous, and appeared to be content. I often wondered how it was like to be blind, or even to be deaf and blind like Helen Keller.

Helen Keller was born in Alabama in 1880. When she was two years old, a serious illness caused her to lose her sight and hearing, which made her unruly. As she would later write; "All the world is full of suffering. It is also full of overcoming." Fortunately, when she was seven, she met her teacher, Anne Sullivan, a graduate of Perkins school for the blind, who taught her how to read and write in Braille. Pretty soon, Helen was able to connect words with objects. For example, as she touched a flower, her teacher would spell this out in her hands.

Then, at the age of thirteen, she was able to perfect her speech. She often said; "The most pathetic person in the world is someone who has sight, but has no vision." What a profound statement; truly a sign of maturation and spiritual insight coming from a blind and deaf person.

Then she entered Radcliffe College at sixteen and graduated with honors in 1904. In her writings, she would point out, "Life is exciting business, and most exciting when it is lived for others. Faith is the strength by which a shattered world shall emerge into the light." This faith she was referring to was her total abandonment to God's holy will. Obviously, Helen although physically blind, had very sharp spiritual eyes. As I said previously, spiritual blindness is the worst kind of blindness. Are there spiritually blind people today?

One time I read about a study made about people who were addicted to digital screens; like cellphone screens, I-Pad screen, TV screens; where they become so engrossed in this digital world that they lose their spiritual insight and perspective. If you mention anything about religion or their faith, they would immediately disengage. If you mention Christianity, they will insist that the subject is irrelevant in today's digital age. However, if you inform them that there are more than two billion Christians around the world who believe in providing assistance and help to needy and hopeless people, they simply ignore the data. Then if you mention to them that without Christian ethics the world would have no vision, no purpose or meaning in life, they turn a deaf ear.

I remember that in the days of Helen Keller, it was Christians who reached out to disabled and handicapped people providing them with trained dogs, help them find jobs, and educate them using the Braille method of reading. Obviously, without Christianity, how dark and blind this world would be. Indeed, how happy are we and those who are not spiritually blind. We know that Jesus Christ, is the way, the truth, and the life. And because of this we can shine and illuminate the darkness of the world to give sight to the spiritually blind. Doing this gives us joy because we are doing God's will.

Divine Intervention

I heard someone say that when God interrupts our lives it has a purpose. This I have often experience in small ways and even in life changing ways. There is really nothing in our experiences that God does not use to help us become better people. His goal is for us to be conformed to his image of love, and the likeness of his Son Jesus. So, let me tell you about Ken, who is a widower, and his experience of being interrupted by God.

His thirty-three-year-old daughter, Joyce, called him one day to inform him that she was pregnant and that her husband had just divorced her. Ken was upset and told Joyce to have an abortion, but Joyce insisted on having her baby. Ken said on the phone, "But you don't have a job, a decent education, or any savings. How can you support a child?"

"God will take care of me," Joyce replied with confidence. Ken was surprised. He had never mentioned God nor religion in the family ever before. He himself was an agnostic and had never been to church.

"Okay, okay, but what is this idea about God taking care of you?" Ken asked.

Joyce mumbled, "I went to church yesterday and talked to the minister about my problem. He sent me to the Crisis Pregnancy Center and a group of churchwomen are counseling me now."

Ken listened, then emphasized, "I'll make a deal with you. I'll accept the idea of your being a mother, but don't ever try to talk me into going to church."

The months that followed, Ken had heard that his daughter got more and more involved with the church, and that she was surviving. Then one day, on New Year's Day, Ken received a phone call from her daughter. "Your grandson is here. Hurry over to my apartment. He'll be ready to meet you in half an hour."

Ken hesitatingly drove to Joyce's apartment.

When the door opened, he was handed a handsome, sleepy six-pound baby boy. When Ken took the baby in his arms, Ken's anger melted, his anxiety evaporated, and his outlook in life changed drastically. Within a week, Ken have moved his daughter and his grandson, George, into his house. New Year's Day that year had never been so wonderful for Ken. The months that followed was the happiest for Ken. Even when Joyce took the baby to church, Ken did not complain or say anything negative about God or the church.

When George was two years old, Ken taught him to walk and how to use the bathroom. They talked about bugs, flowers, and rainbows, and played with a flashlight in the dark. Ken was experiencing transformation without knowing it. Then when George was three years old, Ken took him to ice cream parlors and taught him to sing catchy songs.

One day, as they were strolling along the aisles at a supermarket, and the little boy was standing up in the cart, George started to sing one of his favorite church song about how God is so good.

"So you think God is so good, huh?" Ken asked his grandson.

"Sure, the boy replied.

"And why?" Ken shot back

"Because he made me just for you," came the innocent reply.

Ken was stunned, "He made me just for you." The words echoed in his mind and in his heart. Then he remembered what Joyce said before, "God will take care of me," and at that moment he realized that God did. Suddenly, Ken found himself in deep thought. Before he knew it, he was sincerely thanking God for his daughter

and his special grandson. Then there was a
big smile in his face, as if he had just discovered a special spiritual gem which God has
given him.

Ah, Divine Intervention—it happens all the
time. Some interventions we acknowledge, others
we sometimes call coincidences. But the gift
of a Divine Savior is no coincidence. It was
well orchestrated by God our Father, who will
never abandon us or leave us without hope. He
gave us Jesus as our eternal hope.

As we close this series of Divine
Interventions in this manuscript, as we ponder
the role of the Holy Spirit in shaping our
minds, hearts and souls, we are enchanted by
the following messages:

It all begins with a personal encounter
with God; who is Father, Son, and Holy
Spirit. *The encounter is important.*
The *personal nature* of it is even more
important. It has to be personal. It has
to be a special shared moment with God.
It has to be in the context of prayer
and solitude.

The transcendent moment of the encounter is
like dancing with the stars and lost in eternal
bliss. This singular moment of *falling in love*

with God is beyond words. This moment, this "pearl of great price", this "hidden treasure", will forever be a part of our earthly life. As a mystic once said: Trip over love and you can get up, but *fall in love with God, and you fall forever.* Then you will discover, that there is no remedy to love but to love even more.

It is my hope my dear readers, that your hearts will abandon the cheap allures of the world and the flesh, the quest for fame and fortune, the grabbing of power and control, and instead *seek out the One who has loved you first;* even before you were born. He is the One who wants to write the story of your life, the life He gave you, the life He designed for eternity. Will you let Him?

About the Author

*N*emsy Gubatan was born and educated in the Philippines. As an engineer, he came to the United States to further his education. A traumatic deportation incident proved to be the turning point in his life. He experienced Jesus Christ's personal and unconditional love throughout the deportation trial. Since then, his desire to give back to his "deliverer and rescuer" has involved him in different Parish Ministries. He got involved with the Legion of Mary, the Cursillo Movement, the Kairos Prison Ministry, the Knights of Columbus, and other church organizations.

After pursuing many years of Diaconal Training at the San Pedro Center, he was ordained a Permanent Deacon in the Diocese of Orlando by Bishop Thomas Grady. Currently, he is serving at St. Margaret Mary Church in Winter Park. As an Internet Evangelist, he has maintained the *Practical Spirituality to Be Happy* website. Prior to being a Deacon, he has authored the book *The Secret of Lay Christian Spirituality*. He has also conducted retreats for the Lay Carmelites and provided teachings for Charismatic groups.

CPSIA information can be obtained
at www.ICGtesting.com
Printed in the USA
FFHW010117041218